"*Our Meals* is an easy-to-follow compendium of simple recipes interspersed with p
recollections. . . . What shines throughout the book is the depth of Watts and Soto's
affection for each other. . . . What makes *Our Meals* such a juicy read, too, are its gossipy
asides regarding the high life: dinners at ballet patron Anne Bass's; visits to Bruce Weber's
Adirondack camp; and name-dropping fare like Nora Ephron's Corn Soufflé and the
Fran Lebowitz Dinner, a nod to the evening the sharp-tongued writer insisted on eating
Beluga caviar straight out of the can. Soto and Watts, obviously, have picked up
some of Lebowitz's dry wit."
—*Out* magazine

"New York City Ballet legends Heather Watts and Jock Soto . . . share tips
on throwing memorably festive fêtes in *Our Meals*."
—*Vanity Fair*

"Heather Watts and Jock Soto have defined grace, charm, and elegance. Thank God
they are now the definition of entertaining. I want to eat with them every night."
—Wendy Wasserstein

"Current housemates and former New York City Ballet partners Heather Watts and
Jock Soto share their triumphs and misadventures in the very approachable *Our Meals*."
—*New York* magazine

· · · · ·

Heather Watts danced with the New York City Ballet for twenty-five years, the last
fifteen of them as a principal dancer. She is now a contributing editor at *Vanity Fair*.
Jock Soto has been a principal dancer with the New York City Ballet since 1985, and in 1990 was
named one of *People* magazine's 50 Most Beautiful People. Watts and Soto have danced together
for fifteen years. They have won the March of Dimes Celebrity Food and Wine Award twice, and
have appeared on *CBS Sunday, Today,* the Home Shopping Network, and *Talking Food*.

Our Meals

Making a Home

for Family and Friends

HEATHER WATTS *and* JOCK SOTO

RIVERHEAD BOOKS
New York

RIVERHEAD BOOKS
Published by The Berkley Publishing Group
A member of Penguin Putnam Inc.
375 Hudson Street
New York, New York 10014

Book design by Claire Naylon Vaccaro
Cover design by Lisa Amoroso
Front cover photograph copyright © 1997 by Pat Kepic
Back cover photograph © by Paul Kolnik
Choreography by George Balanchine

First Riverhead hardcover edition: October 1997
First Riverhead trade paperback edition: November 1998
Riverhead trade paperback ISBN: 1-57322-700-5

The Penguin Putnam Inc. World Wide Web site address is
http://www.penguinputnam.com

The Library of Congress has catalogued the Riverhead hardcover edition as follows:

Watts, Heather.
Our meals : making a home for family and friends /
Heather Watts and Jock Soto.
p.   cm
ISBN 1-57322-070-1 (acid-free paper)
1. Cookery. 2. Entertaining. 3. Menus. I. Soto, Jock.
TX714.W285   1997   97-16079 CIP
642'.4—dc21

Printed in the United States of America

10 9 8 7 6 5 4 3 2 1

ACKNOWLEDGMENTS

Thanking the many people who have been meaningful to our shared and separate lives would result in acknowledgments longer than our book! Of course we want to thank everyone—from Mr. Balanchine and Lincoln Kirstein to our teacher Stanley Williams and even the Ford Foundation . . . but this is, after all, a book on entertaining, not on dancing.

We raise a toast to all of the people who shared their recipes with us, the staff at Riverhead Books for their considerable help, Linda Kahn for organizing our thoughts, and Marc and Penelope for looking out for our taste.

An armful of white roses to Susan Petersen for her unflagging enthusiasm. Most of all, we'd like to thank Mary South, our incredibly talented editor and friend, who not only conceived the idea for this book but steadfastly and patiently helped us find the words to both start and finish it.

Since the stories in this book span half a lifetime of shared meals with our families and friends, our greatest wish is that we will one day all share a delicious meal, with the finest of wines, at one very long, candlelit table, laughing and eating together well into the night.

HEATHER WATTS
JOCK SOTO
New York, 1997

Contents

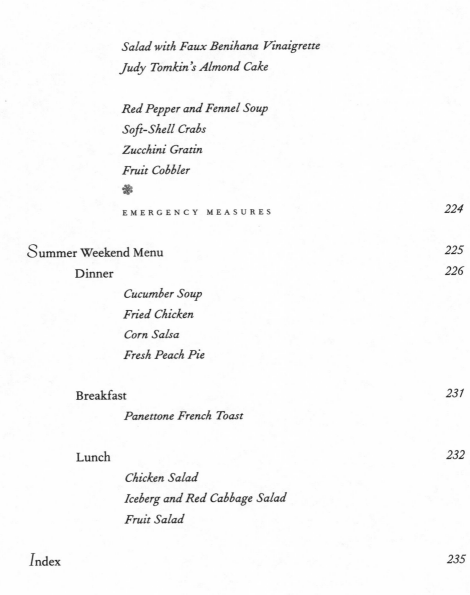

For Damian and Q

If you set out deliberately to make a masterpiece,
how will you ever get it finished?

George Balanchine

INTRODUCTION

Some people seem surprised when they hear that Jock and I are writing a book on entertaining. Perhaps they feel that the "glamour" of an onstage ballet career precludes a home life. Although many people are familiar with our ballet partnership, not everyone knows that we are best friends and that our private life has been as meaningful to us as our careers. In the fifteen years we've known each other, we've passed through many phases, separately and together, but the constant thread in our lives is our friendship. I retired from the New York City Ballet in 1995 after twenty-four years with the company, fifteen of which I danced almost exclusively with Jock. As we stood alone together onstage for the last time, the knowledge that I was losing only a part of our life together gave me strength.

Offstage, that life draws on many of the same qualities that were important to our partnership. Ballet partnerships are rare because they require two people to complement each other's strengths as well as weaknesses, and because they demand a willingness to share the spotlight. In the beginning,

I was the experienced partner, guiding and teaching Jock many tricks of the trade. Nonetheless, in every performance, I was on the receiving end of Jock's innate musicality, virile grace, and brilliant partnering. I grew to rely on him for my every move (literally). Perhaps I danced a little too long, but I loved dancing with Jock so much that it was hard to stop.

Several years ago, Jock, my boyfriend Damian Woetzel, and I bought a house in Washington, Connecticut. Though Jock lives with his boyfriend Christopher Wheeldon a mere forty blocks from Damian and me in the city, our differing schedules make it hard to get together as often as we would like. Every chance we get, though, we head up to our house, where we throw ourselves into cooking, gardening, and all the mundane activities that make a house a home.

Perhaps the best thing about having our house is being able to entertain our family and friends. For one thing, it is an opportunity for Jock and me to work side by side in the kitchen, just as we did onstage. My sister and her family, Jock's parents, and Damian's godfather are all frequent guests, as are our many friends. We drool over the picture-perfect presentations suggested by glossy lifestyle magazines and coffee table cookbooks, but often find ourselves falling a little short. (Who doesn't?) However, our guests don't seem to care.

Our guests are our friends. When they come to our house they know they're going to have good food and lots of laughter. So do we. The real gift of a great meal is more than just the taste of the food—it's the memory of a good time and the sense of home it creates. Our meals have become as much fun for us as they are for our guests—isn't that the secret of entertaining?

H. W.

I.

Learning to Cook

*L*earning to cook is a lot like learning to dance. First you need to learn the rules and techniques. As you gain confidence in your abilities, you will begin to feel that it's okay to break an occasional rule—or maybe add a new one. Just as a gifted dancer uses physical talent and musicality to perform in a unique way, gifted cooks choose and combine ingredients in creative and delicious ways.

Although everyone knows Jock is a great dancer, those who know him well also know that he's a wonderful cook. He started dancing and cooking at an amazingly young age. When he was five, he saw Edward Villella on *The Ed Sullivan Show* and begged his parents to take him to ballet lessons. He started to cook when he was about ten years old. His parents worked, and when he and his brother got home from school, they would fix themselves something to eat using whatever was in the cupboard. Even at this young age, Jock couldn't resist doctoring up their simple snacks. Soon he progressed to making basic pasta dishes and, with his mother's help, Spanish rice, sloppy joes, and other easy family meals.

When he moved to New York in 1980 to study ballet, he shared an apartment with a bunch of other fourteen- and fifteen-year-old students from the School of American Ballet. The filling and inexpensive meals he knew how to make matched their growing-boy appetites as well as their budgets. As Jock's interest in cooking grew, he expanded his repertoire beyond starch by reading cookbooks and food magazines, apprenticing himself to friends who were good cooks, and imitating dishes he tasted in restaurants. After a long day of rehearsing in the theater, he'd often rush home to practice his cooking on friends.

Luckily, I became one of them. In 1970, I had joined the New York City Ballet and moved in with my then boyfriend Peter Martins. Peter and I shared a passion for Balanchine and ballet and an aversion to the kitchen. After our long days of rehearsing, we would rush out to a restaurant. Peter used to tell friends that my idea of making dinner was asking him, "What flavor of yogurt would you like tonight?" Although I wanted to be able to entertain our friends at home, inexperience and fear of failure kept me from trying.

In 1982, Peter paired Jock and me on the stage (in one of his ballets) for the first time. I was an established twenty-eight-year-old ballerina, Jock, at sixteen, was the youngest member of the corps de ballet. Over the next couple of years, our onstage partnership grew and our offstage friendship deepened—often over one of Jock's homemade dinners.

Just as we shared the work onstage, it seemed natural that we begin to share the work offstage. I started with simple tasks—shopping, dicing, cleaning—and we laughingly referred to me as the sous-chef. Spending so many years in the kitchen with Jock has made me a pretty good cook. Now I realize that I missed years of memorable evenings at home with family and friends, all because I was afraid I had to dazzle guests with my culinary expertise. Simple meals can be the most delicious—especially when you share them with people you love. So, don't be afraid to try.

H. W.

EARLY EXPERIMENTS

❋

Meatloaf
Garlicky Smashed Potatoes
Chicken with Forty Cloves of Garlic
Roasted Fennel, Celery Root, and Potatoes

❋

Shortly after I was invited by George Balanchine to join the New York City Ballet in 1980, I moved in with my boyfriend Ulrik Trojaborg, a Danish-born dancer in the company. We rented a two-bedroom apartment in a brownstone on West Eighteenth Street with a relatively large kitchen by New York standards (two people could fit in it at the same time). We fixed the place up, painting and carpeting in shades of black, gray, and white. The decoration was budget Scandinavian—Danish lamps, butterfly chairs, a futon couch. For a dining table, we balanced a piece of plywood on two sawhorses and threw a tablecloth on top.

We entertained a lot in that apartment. I loved having people over and cooking for them. While it was thrilling to be starting my career with the greatest ballet company in the world, I was also a kid in the big city and—sometimes—homesick. Cooking was the way I expressed friendship, and because New Yorkers rarely turn down a home-cooked meal, I not only became popular very quickly but also began to build my new family.

J.S.

Meatloaf

One of the first meals I cooked for Ulrik and our close friend Julia Gruen was meatloaf. It seemed simple—if Alice on *The Brady Bunch* could make it, why couldn't I? I bought ground meat from the butcher, smooshed it up with eggs and lots of herbs and spices, and stuck it in the oven. As I rushed around preparing other dishes and straightening up the apartment, I lost track of time, and completely forgot about the meatloaf.

When Ulrik and Julia arrived three hours later, it was black. With no other option, I transferred the meatloaf to a cutting board and carried it out of the kitchen. Unfortunately, my foot caught on the carpet and the meatloaf went flying, bouncing a couple of times before landing under the dining room table. In a demonstration of true loyalty—or uncontrollable hunger—Ulrik and Julia picked up the meatloaf, dusted it off, and ate what was probably the equivalent of a garlic-flavored loafer. Fifteen years later, they're still two of my best friends.

3½ pounds ground beef chuck

1 small red bell pepper, diced

1 cup bread crumbs

5 eggs

1 teaspoon cumin

2 tablespoons barbecue sauce (My favorite is from the Brooklyn steak house Peter Luger.)

2 tablespoons ketchup

1 tablespoon Dijon mustard

1 small onion, diced

1 tablespoon chopped fresh cilantro (or 1 teaspoon dried)

1 tablespoon chopped fresh thyme or oregano (or 1 teaspoon dried)

3 strips bacon

Preheat oven to 350 degrees.

Mix all of the ingredients except the bacon in a bowl with your hands until well combined. Transfer the mixture to a loaf pan. Lay the bacon strips evenly over the top of the meat.

Bake for 1¼ hours. Remove the meatloaf from the oven and let it stand for 15 minutes before serving.

Don't overcook!

Serves 6.

Garlicky Smashed Potatoes

10 large unpeeled Idaho potatoes, washed and cut into quarters
5 garlic cloves, peeled
4 tablespoons (½ stick) butter
2 cups milk or half-and-half
Salt and pepper

Bring a large pot of water to a boil. Add the potatoes and garlic and boil until the potatoes are soft, about 15 minutes. Drain.

Meanwhile, stir together the butter and either milk or half-and-half in a small saucepan over medium heat until the butter melts.

Mash the potatoes with a potato masher or an electric mixer. Stir in the milk and butter until a creamy but not runny consistency is reached. Add salt and pepper to taste.

Serves 8 to 10.

Chicken with Forty Cloves of Garlic

One of the best ways to avoid the problem of garlic breath embarrassment is simply to make sure everybody present eats some. Truthfully, this isn't as pungent a dish as it sounds, because the garlic bakes for over an hour and loses its sharpness, becoming mellow and sweet. The roasted garlic cloves are delicious smeared on slices of French or Italian bread.

8 pieces of chicken, either a combination of legs and breast-halves or
    2 whole 3-pound chickens cut into quarters
40 or more cloves of garlic, separated from head but not peeled.
4 celery stalks trimmed, sliced in half lengthwise, then cut into 3-inch
    pieces
1 large onion, diced
¼ cup olive oil
1 cup white wine
2 tablespoons chopped fresh tarragon (or 2 teaspoons dried)
Salt and pepper
½ cup half-and-half

Preheat oven to 375 degrees.

Rinse the chicken and pat it dry with paper towels. Place the chicken in a large roasting pan. Add the garlic, celery, onion, olive oil, wine, tarragon, and salt and pepper to taste. Turn the chicken and vegetables to coat them with oil and herbs (I use my hands).

Cover the pan with aluminum foil and, if you have one, a lid. Bake for 1 hour and 15 minutes. Remove the pan from the oven and take off the lid and foil. Stir in the half-and-half, return the pan to the oven, and bake for another 15 minutes uncovered.

Transfer the chicken and vegetables to plates with a slotted spoon. Pass the pan juice separately (it's delicious over white rice).

Serves 8.

Roasted Fennel, Celery Root, and Potatoes

2 fennel bulbs (about 1 pound), trimmed
2 bulbs celery root (about 1 pound), peeled and trimmed
12 red potatoes (about 1 pound), cut in quarters
2 tablespoons olive oil
Salt and pepper

Preheat oven to 375 degrees.

Cut each fennel bulb and celery root into 6 to 8 wedges. Place them in a roasting pan with the potatoes. Drizzle the vegetables with the olive oil, sprinkle with salt and pepper to taste, and turn to coat. Place the roasting pan in the oven and bake, stirring occasionally, for 45 minutes, until the vegetables are golden brown.

Serves 8.

SETTING THE SCENE

Sometimes elevating "having some people over for dinner" to "having a dinner party" can be simple. It doesn't have to take much time, effort, or expense to create a festive, romantic, or elegant setting. A pleasing setting relaxes people and puts them in the mood to appreciate the meal, and can help turn a dinner party into a truly memorable evening.

Here are some ideas for easy, affordable table decoration:

Candles: We place lots of votive and pillar candles around the room, often in unconventional holders. Lit candles on the tabletop is nice, while lighting the whole room using only candles is very dramatic. A couple of tips: Beeswax candles burn slowly and cleanly. A small amount of water at the bottom of votive holders keeps them from being a wax-filled nightmare to clean.

Flowers: One of the great luxuries of life in New York is being able to get inexpensive flowers at every corner deli. I buy bunches of roses or seasonal flowers and put them in warm water to help them open up. Cutting their stems short and placing them in several small vases or even in jam jars can make a table took pretty very quickly. You can also remove the stems entirely and float the flowers in bowls. A bud vase at each place setting with a sprig of fresh herbs is another way to create a stylish and aromatic atmosphere. In Connecticut, when the garden is not in bloom, I find it impossible to buy fresh-cut flowers that aren't ridiculously overpriced, so I'll use a seasonal flowering plant—for instance, hyacinths in the early spring or white poinsettias in the winter.

Centerpieces: Jock often uses fresh vegetables, lemons, oranges, grapes, and even herbs to decorate the center of the table. Whether you use flowers or fruit, remember to keep the centerpieces low enough so that people can talk across the table. I've been lucky enough to be invited to dinner at the White House twice. Once I sat across the table from President Carter and had a wonderful and amusing evening. The Reagans invited me as a guest of honor the second time. Although I sat opposite Mrs. Reagan, I almost couldn't see her because of the gorgeous but obviously much too lavish arrangement of orchids.

Place cards: At any good dinner party, there's a chance some of your guests won't know each other. Place cards are a good way to mastermind new introductions—or sometimes separate old histories! Postcards—new or vintage—make interesting place cards. For Thanksgiving last year, Chris made place cards by collecting fall leaves and writing names on them with glue and glitter. We've amassed a collection of candid Polaroid pictures of all our friends, and months after these funny or embarrassing photos have been forgotten they reappear on the dinner table to mark their places. I'm also always charmed by my friends' children's attempts at spelling guests' names in Crayolas!

Napkins: By now we've accumulated a lot of tablecloths and napkins— some elegant and some less formal. We try to match these to the occasion. For picnics, colorful dishcloths and bandanas are perfect.

Place settings: We try to never worry about mixing tableware or glasses, napkins or silverware. Like all hosts, we sometimes get nervous and wish we had thirty-two matching Baccarat goblets. However, different colors and patterns can lend a lively look to the table.

Holiday meals: We're not even going to suggest the obvious possibilities. Use your imagination. We don't spend hours baking gingerbread houses for Christmas (though we might be tempted to buy one at a charity event). The important thing is a nod to the season or holiday we're celebrating.

GREAT TEACHERS

*C*ookbooks are wonderful, but you can supplement them by watching good cooks on television or in person. I've been fortunate to become friends with a number of people who are excellent chefs and who have shared their knowledge and—as this book attests—their recipes with me. This generosity of spirit may stem from the fact that at heart, cooking is about giving pleasure to others, and people who cook are often deeply flattered when someone shows interest in their art.

I owe many of my cooking techniques to these friends, some of whom have passed away and left me their knowledge and recipes to remember them by. Every time Heather and I make one of their dishes, it brings back great memories of evenings spent eating, drinking, and laughing together. In this way, these friends will always join us for dinner.

J.S.

JANE WILSON

❋

Tandoori-Style Cornish Game Hens
Jane's Shredded Cauliflower
Vegetable Couscous with Onion-Almond-Raisin Sauce
Mesclun Salad with Preserved-Onion Vinaigrette

❋

Julia Gruen's mother, Jane Wilson, is one of the best cooks and greatest teachers I know. For years, Ulrik and I and our colleagues John Bass and Bruce Padgett spent holidays at the Gruens' huge prewar apartment on the Upper West Side. Both Jane and her husband John are artists—she's a renowned painter and he's a well-known writer.

The Gruens always entertain with generosity and great style. As a young dancer in New York, I was dazzled by evenings at their house. We wore jackets and ties and drank fine wines. Hors d'oeuvres often included caviar—the beginning of my addiction. Then we'd move into the dining room, where we enjoyed a magnificent meal. Jane's presentation has always astounded me—she epitomizes elegance, serving beautifully arranged food on gorgeous china, while also casually tossing salads with her hands. After dinner we'd often return to the living room, where Julia played the piano while John ran around posing all of us for photos. This lifestyle was completely new to me and I absorbed everything like a sponge.

Jane is still my culinary mentor—I often call her up when I'm unsure about a recipe or want to try out an idea for a new dish. I've always said that she's the one who ought to write a cookbook. Until she does, here's a sampling of her wonderfully exotic cuisine.

J.S.

Tandoori-Style Cornish Game Hens

*I*f you want the hens to be red, as tandoori-cooked food is in restaurants, add a tablespoon of Patak's tandoori paste to your marinade. Note that you need to begin preparing this dish two days before you want to serve it.

4 1½-pound Cornish game hens	Juice of four limes
2 cups plain yogurt	Kosher salt
2 medium onions, minced	2 tablespoons fresh ginger
2 teaspoons hot or sweet paprika	2 red bell peppers
	Cayenne pepper

DAY 1

Rinse the Cornish hens in cold water and pat them dry. Prick them all over with a fork. Rub them with lime juice and sprinkle lightly with kosher salt. Place each hen in a zip-lock bag and refrigerate overnight.

Place the yogurt in a cheesecloth-lined strainer over a bowl and cover with plastic wrap. Refrigerate overnight.

DAY 2

Puree the ginger, onions, red peppers, paprika, and yogurt in a blender or food processor. Season to taste with cayenne pepper. Distribute the marinade among the four zip-lock bags and massage to coat the hens. Refrigerate overnight.

DAY 3

Preheat oven to 350 degrees

Place the hens in a roasting pan breast side up and cook them for 1 hour, basting occasionally with extra marinade. Turn the heat up to 500 degrees and let the hens brown, basting well, about 10 minutes. Remove the birds from the oven. Let them rest for 10 minutes before serving.

Serves 4.

Jane's Shredded Cauliflower

1 small very fresh head of cauliflower, outer leaves and inner core removed
½ teaspoon cumin
½ red bell pepper, diced fine
½ cup grated carrot
2 shallots, minced.
⅔ cup Hellmann's mayonnaise, crème fraîche, or drained plain yogurt
1 teaspoon celery seeds

Break the cauliflower into florets and place them in a blender or food processor. Add water to cover and pulse to grate. Transfer to a cheesecloth-lined strainer and drain thoroughly.

Place the grated cauliflower in a serving bowl and add the cumin, red pepper, carrot, and shallots. Stir in just enough mayonnaise or crème fraîche or yogurt to bind the vegetables together. Sprinkle with the celery seeds.

Refrigerate until ready to serve.

Serves 8.

Vegetable Couscous with Onion-Almond-Raisin Sauce

4 ounces dark raisins

4 tablespoons (½ stick) unsalted butter

1 pound red onions, sliced thin

¼ teaspoon powdered ginger

½ teaspoon freshly ground black pepper

1 teaspoon cinnamon

2 tablespoons sugar

¼ teaspoon saffron, ground with a mortar and pestle

¾ cup low-sodium or homemade chicken broth

4 ounces blanched whole almonds

Vegetable oil for frying

1 pound couscous

4 cups assorted steamed vegetables of your choice: quartered small turnips, okra, zucchini cut into 1½-inch cubes, carrots cut into bite-sized chucks, broccoli florets, plus canned chick peas, if desired

Soak the raisins for 30 minutes in enough hot water to cover them. Drain.

Meanwhile, melt 2 tablespoons of the butter over low heat in a large saucepan and add the red onions. Cover and cook 10 minutes, until the onions are completely wilted. Stir in the ginger, black pepper, cinnamon, and sugar and half the saffron. Cover and continue cooking for 15 minutes. Add the chicken broth and cook uncovered until the sauce thickens.

In a small skillet, heat the vegetable oil until it's almost smoking. Fry the almonds until they're golden brown. Transfer them to paper towels with a slotted spoon to drain. Add the almonds and raisins to the onion sauce.

Place the couscous in a skillet and toast over medium heat, shaking the pan to ensure that all the grains get browned. Transfer to a large bowl and add 7 cups of boiling water. Let stand 7 to 10 minutes, until all the water is

absorbed, stirring occasionally to break up clumps. Blend the remaining butter and saffron, and stir into the couscous.

Transfer the couscous to the middle of a large serving platter. Arrange the vegetables around the edge and serve the onion-almond-raisin sauce on the side.

Serves 8 to 10.

Mesclun Salad with Preserved-Onion Vinaigrette

*J*ane always has a jar of Moroccan preserved onions in her refrigerator. She uses them in a variety of ways, including this simple yet delectable salad dressing.

2 large onions, sliced thin
Juice of 3 lemons
Salt and pepper
10 cups mesclun or Bibb lettuce or arugula, rinsed and dried
⅓ cup olive oil

Stuff the onion slices into a jar. Cover them with the lemon juice and add a liberal amount of salt and pepper. Close the jar, shake, and refrigerate until the onions start to wilt, about a day and a half. (You can then use these for the next four to five days.)

In a large serving bowl, toss ½ cup of the onions and some juice from the jar with the lettuce and olive oil.

Serves 8.

JOHN BASS

❁

Cassoulet
Orange and Red Onion Salad

❁

John Bass was one of our favorite dinner guests. A longtime dancer in the New York City Ballet, he was much loved for his humor and sharp wit. Among his prize possessions were the complete recordings of Connie Francis and Doris Day, and he loved practical jokes. John lived on good food and imported beer, yet he remained impossibly skinny. Since I've always struggled to keep my weight down, I was mystified by this special quality of his.

John was the first person we knew to die of AIDS. Even this horrifying virus couldn't diminish his sense of humor—he named his rolling IV "Wanda" and claimed that she was stalking him. John was a great-looking guy, but when he lost his hair due to chemotherapy, he felt hats just drew attention to his baldness and, for a while, refused to leave his apartment. Heather decided there was strength in numbers and bought us all baseball caps, which satisfied John's vanity. We still wear them.

Not the least of his many gifts was John's ability to cook. In fact, he was another protégé of Jane Wilson's and had lots to teach me. Here are two of his favorite recipes.

J.S.

Cassoulet

*J*ohn tinkered with this recipe for years—here is the version he left us.

½ pound fresh pork rind

2 pounds dried Great Northern white beans, soaked in water
  overnight

1 5-pound duck

Salt and pepper

1 pound veal bones

2¼ pounds veal stew meat, cut into 1-inch cubes

1 to 2 tablespoons olive oil

2 pounds boneless pork shoulder, cut into 1-inch cubes

1½ tablespoons dried thyme

⅓ cup olive oil

2 cups chopped red onions

3 large carrots, peeled and chopped

3 celery stalks, chopped

2 cups white Zinfandel

6 ounces tomato paste

5 cups low-sodium beef stock

10 garlic cloves, peeled

3 bay leaves

1½ pounds spicy Italian sausage

1 pound salt pork

DAY I

Preheat oven to 450 degrees.

Score the fat side of the pork rind and place it in a small saucepan with water to cover. Bring to a boil, then reduce heat and simmer for 10 minutes. Drain, add fresh cold water to cover, and repeat the process, this time simmering for 30 minutes. Reserve the pork rind and its second cooking water.

Drain the beans and place them in a large ovenproof pot with enough fresh water to cover. Bring to a boil, reduce heat, and cook uncovered for 15 minutes. Remove the pot from the heat and let the beans stand in their cooking liquid.

Rinse the duck in cold water, pat dry, and trim off any excess fat. Cut off the wing tips and remove and discard neck, heart, and gizzards. Season the duck with salt and pepper to taste, inside and out. Place the duck in one roasting pan and the veal bones in another, and roast for 45 minutes, siphoning the fat from the duck pan frequently. Remove both pans from the oven and reduce the heat to 350 degrees. The duck will be a little underdone, but the veal bones should be browned. Cool the duck, cover with foil, and put in the fridge.

In a heavy skillet brown the cubed veal in batches, seasoning to taste with salt and pepper, and set aside in a bowl. Without cleaning the skillet, pour in the 1 to 2 tablespoons olive oil and sauté the cubed pork and wing tips, neck, and giblets of the duck, adding the thyme, and salt and pepper to taste. Transfer to the bowl with the cubed veal.

Pour the ⅓ cup olive oil into the same skillet, then add the onions, carrots, and celery, and sauté for 20 minutes. Add the vegetables to the pot with the cooked beans in water.

Into the skillet now pour the Zinfandel along with any meat juice that has accumulated in the bowl. Bring to a boil, lower the heat slightly, and cook briskly until the wine is reduced by half.

Pour the contents of the skillet into the bean pot. Stir in the tomato paste, beef stock, 6 garlic cloves, and the bay leaves, and the combined veal, pork, and duck from the bowl. Add water if necessary to cover the contents and place the pork rind on top, fat side down. Cover the pot and place in the oven. Bake for 2 to 2½ hours, until the beans are tender. Remove the pot from the oven, uncover, and cool to room temperature, stirring occasionally. Cover and refrigerate overnight.

Prick the sausage all over with a fork and simmer it in a pan of water for 30 minutes. Drain and save.

Place the salt pork in a pan of cold water, then bring it to a boil and cook for 10 minutes. Drain, cover with fresh cold water, and repeat, leaving the pork to cook in the cooking water.

Remove the beans from the refrigerator. Discard the veal bones.

Drain the salt pork and trim and discard the rind. Chop the salt pork into cubes and puree it in a food processor along with the remaining garlic cloves. Stir the pureed mixture into the beans.

Remove the duck from the refrigerator, skin it, and remove all the meat from the bones. Cut the meat into bite-sized chunks and stir them into the beans. Cook the beans over medium heat, covered, for 1½ hours. If they become dry, add water.

Meanwhile, preheat oven to 325 degrees.

Uncover the beans and bake for 45 minutes until a crust forms. Serve immediately.

Serves 12.

Orange and Red Onion Salad

6 oranges, peeled and separated into segments
2 medium red onions, sliced thin
4 tablespoons olive oil
2 tablespoons red wine vinegar
1 tablespoon chopped fresh mint
1 teaspoon red pepper flakes
Salt and pepper
1 tablespoon chopped fresh chives

Remove the membrane from the orange segments with a sharp paring knife, collecting the juices and placing the trimmed segments in a medium serving bowl. Add the red onion slices, olive oil, vinegar, mint, and red pepper flakes to the bowl and toss to combine. Add salt and pepper to taste. Top with the chives. Refrigerate and serve cold.

Serves 8.

JOHN BEAL

❄

Asparagus Risotto
Roasted Pork Loin with Herbs
Mashed Parsnips and Carrots
Watercress Salad
Lemon Tart

❄

When I met John Beal, he had been performing modern dance with a variety of companies in New York for many years and was beginning to suffer burnout. Soon afterward he decided to embark on a new career as a model, packed his bags, and moved to Paris. There, in the birthplace of fine cuisine, his appreciation of good food developed into an obsession. While modeling he studied cooking, and after two years, returned to New York.

At first John took a few jobs in catering shops to supplement his modeling income, but eventually gave up modeling to become a full-time chef. In addition to making food, he often styled it for magazines and advertising shoots.

Sadly, John also died of AIDS, and for a while I lived in complete despair. Perhaps as part of my healing process, I began to borrow his *eye* for food. From John Beal, I learned not only how to cook but how to achieve picture-perfect presentation.

J.S.

Asparagus Risotto

5 to 6 cups low-sodium or homemade chicken broth

3 tablespoons olive oil

1 large onion, chopped

24 asparagus spears, trimmed and cut in half lengthwise

1½ tablespoons chopped fresh thyme (or 1½ teaspoons dried)

Salt and pepper

1½ cups arborio rice

2 tablespoons unsalted butter

½ cup grated Parmesan cheese

Bring the chicken broth to a boil in a medium saucepan, then cover and simmer.

In a large heavy pot heat the olive oil. Add the onion, asparagus, thyme, salt and pepper to taste, and stir over medium heat for 5 minutes. Add the rice and stir to coat with oil. Increase the heat and add about ½ cup of the broth to rice, stirring constantly. As soon as the stock has been absorbed, add another ½ cup of broth and stir again, so the rice doesn't stick to the pot. Continue adding the broth, ½ cup at a time, until the rice is cooked and creamy, about 20 minutes.

Remove the pan from the heat and stir in the butter and half the Parmesan cheese. Serve immediately, with the remaining cheese on the side.

Serves 10 to 12 as an appetizer, or 6 as a main course.

Roasted Pork Loin with Herbs

1 3-pound pork loin, boned but not tied (Ask the butcher for string,
    as you will need it later.)
5 garlic cloves, minced
½ tablespoon chopped fresh thyme (or ½ teaspoon dried)
½ tablespoon chopped fresh rosemary (or ½ teaspoon dried)
3 tablespoons olive oil
Salt and pepper

Preheat oven to 350 degrees.

Rinse the pork loin in cold water and pat it dry. In a small bowl, combine the garlic, thyme, and rosemary with 1 tablespoon of the olive oil. Spread the mixture inside the pork loin. Roll the loin like a jelly roll and tie it firmly in three or four places, several inches apart. Slather the remaining olive oil on the pork and sprinkle generously with pepper.

Place the pork in a roasting pan and bake for approximately 1 hour, until the meat is only a little pink inside. Remove it from the oven, sprinkle with salt if desired, and cover with aluminum foil to allow it to continue cooking for 10 more minutes. Carve and serve hot or at room temperature.

Serves 6.

Mashed Parsnips and Carrots

1½ pounds carrots (about 6 medium-sized), peeled and cut into
    ½-inch rounds
2 pounds parsnips, peeled and cut into ½-inch rounds
4 tablespoons (½ stick) unsalted butter
½ cup low-sodium or homemade chicken broth
Ground nutmeg
Salt and pepper

Place the carrots in a large pot of boiling salted water, cover partially, and simmer for 5 minutes. Add the parsnips, cover partially, and simmer until the vegetables are tender, about 15 minutes (test with a fork). Drain the vegetables and transfer to the bowl of an electric mixer. Add the butter and beat until pureed, thinning with the chicken broth until creamy but not runny. Season to taste with nutmeg and salt and pepper.

Serves 6 to 8.

Watercress Salad

⅓ cup Preserved-Onion Vinaigrette (see page 19)
2 tablespoons olive oil
1 teaspoon Dijon mustard
Salt and pepper
3 bunches watercress, trimmed, washed, and dried

Place the Preserved-Onion Vinaigrette, olive oil, and mustard in the bottom of a salad bowl. Lightly whisk. Add salt and pepper to taste. Add the watercress and toss, and serve immediately (watercress tends to wilt quickly).

Serves 6.

Lemon Tart

CRUST

　1 to 1¼ cups flour

　7 tablespoons unsalted butter, chilled and cut into pieces

　2 teaspoons sugar

　⅛ teaspoon salt

　3 tablespoons ice water

Place one cup of flour and the butter, sugar, and salt in the bowl of a food processor fitted with a metal blade. Process just until the mixture resembles coarse crumbs, about 10 seconds. Add the water little by little, slowly pulsing after each addition, until the pastry begins to hold together (you may not need all 3 tablespoons of water, but you certainly won't need more).

　The second the dough forms a ball, stop processing and turn it out onto waxed paper. Mold it into a biscuit shape. If the dough is excessively sticky, sprinkle with a tablespoon or two of flour. Wrap it in waxed paper and refrigerate for at least one hour.

FILLING

　Grated rind of 2 lemons

　¾ cup sugar

　¾ cup lemon juice

　4 eggs, lightly beaten

In a large bowl, whisk everything together.

ASSEMBLY

　Preheat oven to 350 degrees.

　Remove the dough from the refrigerator and roll it out to ⅛-inch thickness on a well-floured surface. Transfer to a 10-inch fluted tart pan with a removable bottom. Press the dough into the corners of the pan and trim the edges (the easiest way to do this is to roll the pin across the top of the fluted edges, neatly cutting off the overhang). Place dried beans or pie weights in the center of the dough and bake for 10 minutes.

Take the shell out of the oven and remove the weights. Carefully pour the filling into the shell and bake for 35 minutes, until set. Garnish as you like.

Serves 8.

A Word on Wine

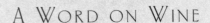

One of the lovely perks of being a ballet dancer is that we frequently get gifts of great champagne. In fact, this happens so often that we have never developed a hoarding mentality. We'll open a gorgeous bottle of champagne with friends just to celebrate being together!

We're also wine lovers, but not wine experts. When you entertain as much as we do, it's a good idea to develop some affordable favorites. For everyday meals, we try to keep ourselves in the $10 range, although some good wines are available for even less than that.

We love St.-Emilion—Château Le Loup is our everyday brand, and when we're celebrating, Château Simmard. These are rich, full reds that go well with grilled meats and heavier meals. I love Riojas with beef and chicken. Rodney Strong makes a wonderful Cabernet which is also great with chicken. Pizza and pasta scream for Chianti, but a light red like Beaujolais is also delicious.

In the summer, like most Americans, we drink more white wine. We're fond of the Woodbridge White Zinfandel, which is a nice, spicy, light blush wine perfect for outdoor meals. I also like a crisp, dry Italian Pinot Grigio, while Jock leans toward an oaky American Chardonnay.

There are really no rules about which wines go best with which foods, and most of the time we serve whatever our guests bring us without worrying too much about suitability. No one has complained yet.

MICHAEL JAMES

❃

Chicken Pot Pie
Omelet with Rosemary, Truffles, and Parmesan Cheese
Pizza with Pancetta, Herbs, and Cheese

❃

Years ago, Heather, Peter Martins, Peter's son Nilas, Ulrik, and I were invited to our friends Courtney and Steve Ross's home in East Hampton for Christmas. As the head of Time Warner, Steve Ross lived in incredible luxury in a truly beautiful home. He was remarkably generous and enjoyed sharing his good fortune with others. Courtney is one of the greatest hostesses—relaxed, calm, and incredibly welcoming.

On this memorable holiday, we ate one fantastic meal after another. Heather and I *had* to meet the chef, so Courtney took us into the kitchen and introduced us to the remarkable Michael James. We spent most of our time in the kitchen from then on, shadowing Michael and learning all that we could. We all became good friends, and to this day we toast him every time we make a recipe that he inspired.

J.S.

Chicken Pot Pie

PASTRY

> ¾ pound (3 sticks) chilled unsalted butter, cut into 1-inch pieces
>
> 3 cups flour
>
> 1 teaspoon salt
>
> ⅔ cup ice water

Place the butter, flour, and salt in the bowl of a large food processor (if your machine isn't big enough, work in batches). Pulse until combined, then add the water, a couple of tablespoons at a time, until the crumbs just begin to come together. Generously flour your work surface, then pour out the dough and roll it into a 6-x-18-inch rectangle. With a spatula, fold the dough in half, then in half again. Reroll, adding more flour if the dough begins to get sticky. Fold in half once again, wrap in plastic wrap, and refrigerate for 1 hour. Remove the dough from the fridge, roll again, fold again, and chill for another hour or until ready to use.

FILLING

> 1 3-pound chicken, quartered, plus 2 breasts
>
> 6 tablespoons olive oil
>
> Salt and pepper
>
> 2 large Idaho potatoes, peeled or unpeeled
>
> 20 pearl onions
>
> 4 large carrots
>
> 6 garlic cloves, peeled
>
> 12 button mushrooms
>
> 4 tablespoons chopped fresh herbs (any combination of rosemary, sage, thyme, and oregano)
>
> ¾ cup peas, fresh or frozen
>
> ¾ cup corn, fresh or frozen
>
> 6 tablespoons flour
>
> 4 cups low-sodium or homemade chicken broth

Preheat oven to 375 degrees.

Rinse the chicken parts in cold water and pat them dry. Rub the chicken with 1 tablespoon of olive oil and sprinkle with salt and pepper. In a roasting pan, toss the potatoes, onions, carrots, garlic, mushrooms, and herbs with 2 tablespoons of olive oil. Place the chicken parts on top and roast for 1 hour and 15 minutes, stirring occasionally. Remove the chicken from the pan and set aside to cool. Transfer the vegetables to a bowl and add the peas and corn.

Without rinsing the roasting pan, place it on the stove and in it warm the remaining 3 tablespoons olive oil over medium heat. When it is bubbling, add the flour and stir, scraping up any brown bits that are stuck to the pan. When there are no more lumps, slowly add the broth and salt and pepper to taste, and whisk for about 15 minutes until a gravy forms.

When the chicken is cool enough to handle, remove the meat from the bones, add it to the vegetables, and stir to combine. Transfer the chicken and vegetables to a 9-x-13-inch ovenproof casserole dish, add the gravy, and mix everything together.

ASSEMBLY

1 egg yolk
2 tablespoons heavy cream

Preheat oven to 400 degrees.

Remove the dough from the refrigerator and roll it out large enough to fit over the casserole dish. Drape the dough over the casserole and pinch the edges to the sides of the dish to seal.

In a small bowl combine the egg yolk and heavy cream with a fork. Brush the dough with the wash, then bake the casserole for 50 to 60 minutes, until the top is golden brown.

Serves 8.

Omelet with Rosemary, Truffles, and Parmesan Cheese

8 eggs
2 tablespoons chopped fresh rosemary, plus sprigs for garnish
¼ cup half-and-half
Salt and pepper
2 tablespoons (¼ stick) unsalted butter
½ medium red onion, diced very fine
¼ cup grated Parmesan cheese
Shaved truffles

In a bowl whisk the eggs with the rosemary, half-and-half, and salt and pepper to taste.

Melt the butter in a large frying pan and sauté the onion over medium heat until translucent, about 5 minutes. Add the egg mixture to the pan and cook until the bottom of the omelet begins to brown, about 7 minutes. Sprinkle with the cheese and a few shavings of truffles, then with a spatula fold the omelet in half. Cook about 5 minutes longer.

Divide the omelet into four pieces and serve hot with a garnish of fresh rosemary and a few more shavings of truffles.

Serves 4.

Pizza with Pancetta, Herbs, and Cheese

*N*ow that we spend weekends in the country, a hundred miles from our favorite New York pizzerias, I find myself making pizza from scratch fairly often. Of course, the toppings can be varied to suit your mood and what's available.

CRUST

> 1 package dry yeast
> 1 cup warm water (105 to 110 degrees)
> 3½ cups flour
> 1 teaspoon salt
> 2 tablespoons olive oil

Dissolve the yeast in warm water and let it stand for 5 to 10 minutes. In a large mixing bowl combine the flour and salt. Make a well in the center of the dry ingredients, then add half of the yeast-water, mixing it with your hands. Add the olive oil, continue mixing, then add the rest of the yeast-water, continuing to mix until all the flour is incorporated (if necessary, add a little more water). Turn the dough out onto a flat surface and knead it vigorously for 10 minutes. Shape it into a ball and place it in an oiled bowl. Cover it with a damp cloth and let it rise until double in bulk, for 1 to 2 hours. Punch the dough down and divide it in half.

ASSEMBLY

> Cornmeal for dusting the pizza stone or baking sheet
> 3 tablespoons olive oil for rubbing the dough
> 4 cups grated mozzarella cheese—fresh, not from a bag!
> 2 pounds ripe tomatoes, sliced ¼-inch thick
> ¼ pound pancetta, diced
> 6 garlic cloves, minced
> 6 sage sprigs, chopped
> 3 tablespoons chopped fresh thyme

1 large red onion, sliced wafer thin
¾ cup grated Parmesan cheese
Salt and pepper

Preheat oven to 450 degrees.

Roll each dough ball out on a floured surface until it's approximately 18 inches in diameter. Transfer it to a pizza stone or baking sheet that has been generously sprinkled with cornmeal (the easiest way to do this is to fold the dough circle in half, move it, then unfold it on the surface). Rub the dough with olive oil

Divide the remaining ingredients and arrange them on top of the pizzas. Bake each pie for 18 to 20 minutes, until the crust is lightly browned.

Serves 8.

LARZ ANDERSON

❊

Spicy Ginger and Carrot Soup
Grilled Swordfish with Tomato Concasse and Eggplant

❊

Larz Anderson's life always seemed so thrilling. He'd pick us up in his convertible and we'd go driving. He once tried to take us to this famous Greek restaurant in Queens, but when we arrived it was closed. We didn't really mind—we were just so happy to be zooming around the city with the top down. Larz was a huge fan of the ballet, and every time he came to a performance he'd invite us to dinner afterward.

Larz lived right next door to Bruce Padgett. Whenever I'd visit Bruce, I'd pop in and say hello to Larz. One day I remember peeking through Bruce's window and seeing Larz making dinner. I banged on the window and screamed, "What are you making and why didn't you invite me?"

Larz was a fantastic cook. One year for Christmas he gave all his friends copies of a little self-published book called *Larz's Tomato Cookbook,* which included his favorite recipes and photos of him cooking them. We never actually had the chance to cook with Larz, but I'm sure it would have been as much fun as riding in his blue Miata.

J.S.

Spicy Ginger and Carrot Soup

1 tablespoon unsalted butter
1 large onion, diced
4 large garlic cloves
8 large carrots, peeled and cut into pieces
1 large Idaho potato, peeled and cut into chunks
1½ tablespoons chopped fresh ginger
1 tablespoon fresh thyme (or 1 teaspoon dried)
½ teaspoon dried cumin
½ teaspoon curry powder
6 cups low-sodium or homemade chicken broth
Juice of 1 lemon
Salt and pepper

In a large stockpot, melt the butter and sauté the onion and garlic over medium heat for 5 minutes, until the onion is translucent. Add the carrots, potato, ginger, thyme, cumin, and curry powder. Cook for approximately 15 minutes over low heat, stirring occasionally. Add the broth and lemon juice, cover, and simmer for 30 minutes.

Puree the soup in a blender or food processor, or with a hand-held blender. Return it to the pot and add salt and pepper to taste. Keep warm on low heat, stirring occasionally until ready to serve.

Serves 6 to 8.

Grilled Swordfish with Tomato Concasse and Eggplant

HERB MAYONNAISE

    4 large egg yolks
    ½ teaspoon salt
    5 tablespoons lemon juice
    1½ to 2 cups olive oil
    3 tablespoons chopped fresh rosemary (or 3 teaspoons dried, soaked in
        water)
    2 tablespoons anchovy paste

Place the yolks, salt, and half the lemon juice in a bowl and whisk until smooth. Whisk in the oil, very slowly at first, increasing the flow at the end. If the mayonnaise gets too thick to beat, add droplets of water, then continue adding oil until creamy. Whisk in the remaining lemon juice. Mix in the rosemary and anchovy paste. Cover with plastic wrap and refrigerate.

TOMATO CONCASSE

    2 large summer tomatoes
    ½ cup mixed chopped fresh herbs, such as basil, marjoram, tarragon,
        or thyme (or 1½ tablespoons dried)
    2 large shallots, chopped
    ½ cup fresh lemon juice or white wine vinegar
    1 cup olive oil

Peel and seed the tomatoes. (To peel, drop the tomatoes in boiling water for 5 seconds or until the peel starts splitting. Remove them and immerse immediately in ice water for 30 seconds. The peels will slip off.) Dice the tomatoes and drain them in a small strainer set over a bowl. Transfer to a bowl, add the herbs, shallots, lemon juice, or vinegar and olive oil, and toss to blend. Set aside.

ASSEMBLY

    8 8-ounce pieces of swordfish, 1 inch thick

    1 cup olive oil

    2 tablespoons chopped fresh thyme (or 2 teaspoons dried)

    2 tablespoons chopped fresh marjoram (or 2 teaspoons dried)

    16 medium Japanese eggplants or baby purple eggplants

    2 sprigs fresh rosemary, chopped (or 1 teaspoon dried)

    8 teaspoons mayonnaise (for garnish)

Fire up the grill or preheat the broiler.

Rinse the swordfish under cold water and pat dry with paper towels. Place the fish in a single layer in a shallow baking dish. Combine ½ cup of the olive oil with the thyme and marjoram and pour over the fish. Turn to coat, and marinate for 30 minutes.

Cut the eggplants in half, if small, or ½-inch-thick slices if large, and marinate in the remaining olive oil and the rosemary for 30 minutes.

Grill the eggplant first, for about 5 minutes on each side, then move them to the side of the grill. If broiling, broil on both sides until tender and brown, then place them on a warm platter.

Cook the fish over the hottest part of the fire or in the broiler for 5 to 6 minutes on each side until medium rare.

Distribute the fish and eggplant among eight warm plates. Spoon the tomato concasse on top of the fish and put a dollop of mayonnaise on top of that. Pass the extra sauce at the table.

Serves 8.

II.

City Cuisine

New York is a food lover's paradise. There are so many restaurants serving such varied and delicious cuisine from all over the world that it's tempting to eat out—or order in all the time. More and more, however, we find ourselves choosing to eat and entertain at home.

Dinner parties provide a great opportunity to try new recipes and experiment with exotic ingredients. We live surrounded by fabulous gourmet stores and green markets, a side of New York people who don't cook can never fully appreciate. Just browsing through them is an inspiration—ten different kinds of olive oil, huge bunches of fresh herbs, a rainbow array of fresh pastas, hundreds of cheeses, mushrooms with names you can't even pronounce. An ingredient bought spur-of-the-moment can often end up being the centerpiece of a delicious new invention.

Sharing meals with friends in your own home also lends a special warmth and intimacy to the evening that you can't achieve in most public places. A home-cooked meal is a unique gift of your own time and creativity, one that is particularly appreciated in a world where everyone's always

in a rush. Plenty of times *we're* in a rush and stressed out and thinking there's no way we'll be able to throw a dinner party on top of all our other commitments, and maybe we'd better just eat out. But when the guests arrive and the meal is served, we're always glad we made the effort. And so are our friends.

H. and J.

CHELSEA DINNER PARTY

❄

Pasta with Vegetable Sauce and Sautéed Chanterelles
Lemon Chicken
Pattypan Squash
Arugula with Parmesan Cheese and Tangy Vinaigrette

❄

After three years in a floor-through on Eighteenth Street, Ulrik and I moved to Twenty-first Street, to a beautiful apartment that we couldn't afford. In spite of the fact that we were headed straight toward financial destruction, we were very excited and thought, Why not throw a party? By the time I had finished inviting people, there were twenty names on our guest list. We were in a rehearsal period at the time, so I hoped that I might have the day of the party off. Wishful thinking! I wound up having rehearsal from noon to six, and the dinner guests were due to arrive at eight.

Still, I figured I could shop in the morning, then cook between six and eight. But to make matters worse, I overslept on the day of the dinner party and woke up too late to do anything but pull on some jeans and dash to the theater. I was in a panic. Luckily, my last rehearsal was canceled, so I phoned Ulrik and asked him if he could get the house prepared and buy flowers and ice. Then I ran to Balducci's. Legendary for its selection of gourmet food, Balducci's is the kind of place where people contemplate each sprig of parsley—not the place to go in a rush. I planned my attack, leaving my cart behind while I dodged leisurely shoppers inching down the aisles and indecisive customers fondling their Anjou pears. After battling the crowd, I made it home with four chickens, lemons, vegetables, fresh pasta, salad items, cheese, and store-bought tarts. (Making dessert from scratch would have put me over the edge!)

By this time it was about six-thirty. Because the chickens take longest to cook, the first thing I had to do was get them washed, seasoned, and in the oven. Then I prepared the pattypan squash, leaving them in a pan on the stove, ready to be fired up at the last minute. Next I cut up carrots, celery, tomatoes, onions, potatoes, and garlic, added a little broth, and cooked and blended everything into a vegetable sauce for the pasta appetizer. *And* washed the salad.

Time to set the table. Our usual table seated twelve at most, so we brought the desk from the office into the living room and set places for twenty. The plates, glasses, and napkins were all mismatched, but strategically placed so that each setting matched the one across from it. Postcards made great place cards. Dozens of votive candles lit up the room. With a couple of bunches of flowers from the corner deli, we ended up with a beautiful, creative, yet inexpensive table.

When the guests arrived they were offered a drink and a selection of cheeses arranged on the coffee table. Meanwhile, I was sweating it out in the kitchen, trying desperately to remain under control. This is *not* my favorite way to throw a dinner party, but sometimes you have no choice. It's good to know that if you keep the meal simple, you can pull off a semi-elegant affair under less than ideal circumstances.

Dinner was served at nine, and I'm told it was delicious. After the unbelievable day I'd had, exhaustion took over. I sat in a pleasant daze at the head of the table and enjoyed watching everyone eat.

J.S.

Pasta with Vegetable Sauce and Sautéed Chanterelles

5 tablespoons olive oil
4 carrots, peeled and diced
3 celery stalks, diced
1 Idaho potato, peeled and diced
1½ medium Spanish onions, diced (about 2 cups)
6 garlic cloves, minced
5 large tomatoes, diced
2 cups low-sodium or homemade chicken broth
Salt and pepper
16 ounces linguine
8 chanterelle mushrooms, dusted off with a paper towel, not washed
Parmesan cheese

Heat 1 tablespoon of the olive oil in a large heavy saucepan or skillet. Place all the vegetables in the pan and cook over medium heat for 15 minutes, or until soft. Add the chicken broth and bring to a boil. Simmer for 15 minutes, uncovered. Remove from the heat and puree in a blender or food processor, or with a hand-held blender. Return the sauce to the pan and add salt and pepper to taste. Cover and keep warm over low flame.

Bring a large pot of water to a boil with 2 tablespoons of the olive oil. Cook the linguine according to the package directions. Meanwhile, heat the remaining 2 tablespoons of olive oil in a medium skillet. Sauté the chanterelles for three minutes. Drain the linguine and add it to the vegetable sauce, stirring until the pasta is thoroughly coated. Transfer to plates, topping each portion with one mushroom. Sprinkle with freshly grated Parmesan cheese.

Serves 8 as an appetizer, or 4 as a main course.

Lemon Chicken

*T*he first time I tasted this chicken must have been when Ulrik made it in our Eighteenth Street apartment. We had bought Marcella Hazan's *Classic Italian Cookbook* and there it was—the easiest, fastest, and cheapest way to make chicken. She simply salts and peppers the chicken inside and out, then sticks two lemons that have been punctured twenty times inside the cavity, ties it up, and puts it in the oven. An hour and a half later it's ready to eat. But I, of course, had to add a few more goodies.

    2 whole chickens, 3½ to 4 pounds each
    Salt and pepper
    10 garlic cloves, peeled and left whole
    4 lemons, poked 20 times each with a skewer
    6 to 8 sprigs of fresh thyme
    2 cups white wine, low-sodium chicken broth, or water
    String to truss the chicken (Heather and I always forget this. Some
        creative alternatives we've tried include a safety pin and paper
        clips. Once she offered a toe-shoe ribbon, but we decided not to
        risk starting a fire.)

Preheat oven to 400 degrees.

Wash the chickens inside and out with cold water, removing the gizzards and whatever else is in that little bag inside the cavity. Pat them dry with a paper towel. Salt and pepper generously inside and out. Stick the garlic, lemons, and thyme in the cavities and truss the chickens as well as you can so everything stays inside.

Place chickens directly in a large roasting pan, breast side up. Fill the pan with about an inch of the white wine, chicken broth, or water (I prefer wine). Place the chickens in the oven. After 15 minutes, take them out and turn them over, then cook for another 20 minutes. Take them out and turn them over again (back to breast side up), turn the heat down to 350 degrees, and bake for another 45 minutes, basting every 15 minutes, until brown. If the liquid at the bottom of the pan evaporates, add water. To test whether the chickens are done, pierce a leg with a sharp knife; the juices should run clear. Remove the chickens from the oven and let them stand for 10 minutes.

Serves 8.

Pattypan Squash

1½ pounds yellow pattypan squash
1½ pounds green baby zucchini
4 tablespoons unsalted butter (½ stick)
5 garlic cloves, crushed
1 tablespoon chopped fresh thyme (or 1 teaspoon dried)
1 tablespoon chopped fresh rosemary (or 1 teaspoon dried)
Salt and pepper

Scrub the pattypan squash and zucchini gently with a vegetable brush under cold water and dry thoroughly. If the squash are much bigger than the zucchini, cut them in half so all the vegetables are approximately the same size.

Melt the butter in a large skillet. Add the squash, zucchini, garlic, herbs, and salt and pepper to taste. Cover the skillet with a lid and sauté over medium heat until the squash are cooked but still firm, 10 to 15 minutes. Serve immediately.

Serves 8.

Arugula with Parmesan Cheese and Tangy Vinaigrette

¼ cup olive oil
2 tablespoons balsamic vinegar
½ tablespoon Dijon mustard
Salt and pepper
3 bunches fresh arugula, washed well (it's often very sandy) and dried
4 ounces Parmesan cheese

In a small jar mix the olive oil, vinegar, mustard, and salt and pepper to taste. Cover and shake vigorously. Place the arugula in a large salad bowl and add the vinaigrette, turning to coat thoroughly. Shave curls of Parmesan cheese on top using a vegetable peeler. Toss again and serve.

Serves 8.

Instant Desserts

*M*aybe it's because there are so many distractions in the city, but for some reason, we often find ourselves scrambling to throw together dinner parties at the last minute. One thing this doesn't usually allow us to do is make homemade desserts. Fortunately, there are a lot of wonderful bakeries where we can pick up dessert. While we never claim credit for them when asked directly, we don't advertise the fact that they're not baked from scratch.

Here are some other suggestions for instant desserts:

Chocolates and cookies

Italian biscotti

Ice cream topped with liqueur, such as amaretto, Kahlúa, brandy, or crème de cacao

Fruit-flavored sorbet with fresh berries

Mixed berries marinated in a splash of fruit-flavored liqueur, such as kirsch or Grand Marnier, or with heavy cream (or both!)

Homemade ice cream sandwiches: Place a scoop of ice cream between two big store-bought cookies, roll in sprinkles, chopped nuts, or chocolate chips, wrap in waxed paper, and freeze.

Rum-soaked pound cake: Poke holes in the top of a store-bought pound cake with a toothpick and drizzle with rum. Wrap in plastic wrap and marinate overnight.

And don't forget! Cheese and fruit is always a great way to end a meal.

PRINCIPAL PORK DINNER

❋

Principal Pork
Apple-Cranberry Relish
Nora Ephron's Corn Soufflé
Damian's Bananas Foster

❋

One night in October 1985, I stopped in the butcher's on the way home from rehearsal and bought a loin of pork. I was making dinner for Heather, Peter (by then the director of the New York City Ballet), and Ulrik. I wasn't sure exactly what I would do with the pork, but it looked good and I knew it wouldn't take too long to cook.

Heather was waiting in my apartment when I got home. After we unpacked the groceries she called Peter, who was still at the theater. They talked, and at one point in the conversation Heather let out this little yelp. She hung up and didn't explain anything. I heard her whispering to Ulrik in the other room, but I was busy with dinner and didn't think much about it.

About a half an hour later, Peter arrived. He handed me a magnum of champagne and said, "Congratulations, I've promoted you to principal dancer!" For a split second I think I went into shock—I just felt numb, as if time had stopped. Then the news sank in. I put the bottle down on the table and ran to the phone to call my parents.

They were as excited as I was. Being promoted to principal is the crowning achievement of a dancer's career. It's the dream that keeps you going through the long hours of practice, through the pain of injuries, the frustration of disappointing performances. At twenty, I not only was the youngest principal dancer in the world's greatest ballet company, but had been paired with the ballerina of my dreams in the masterworks of Balanchine, Robbins, and Martins.

When I got off the phone, Peter popped the cork. We had a champagne toast, then sat down to eat. To this day, that evening is one of my happiest memories, not only because I was promoted, but because I was able to celebrate my good fortune with my closest friends. We christened the feast "Principal Pork," and have enjoyed this delectable recipe countless times over the years.

J.S.

Principal Pork

3 pounds pork loin, boned but not tied (Ask the butcher for string,
   as you'll need it later.)
1 teaspoon cumin
1 tablespoon chopped fresh thyme (or 1 teaspoon dried)
5 garlic cloves, minced
2 tablespoons olive oil
½ cup orange juice
½ cup red wine
Salt and pepper

Preheat oven to 350 degrees.

Trim any excess fat off of the pork, rinse it in cold water, and pat it dry
with paper towels. Season generously with pepper, then massage the cumin,
thyme, and garlic all over the loin. Tie it up into a long log and coat it with
the olive oil.

Place the pork in a roasting pan with the orange juice and red wine. (If
you want to save yourself some heavy scrubbing later, line the pan with aluminum foil.) Cook for 1 hour. The roast is done when a meat thermometer
reads 160 degrees and the loin is only a little pink inside. Remove it from the
oven, sprinkle with salt if desired, and allow it to rest for 10 minutes, tented
with aluminum foil. The pork may be eaten hot or at room temperature.

Serves 6.

Apple-Cranberry Relish

½ cup dried cranberries
1 tablespoon unsalted butter
4 teaspoons sugar
1½ cups tart green apples, such as Granny Smith (about 1 medium
 apple), peeled and diced
3 tablespoons chopped red onion
2 tablespoons lemon juice
2 teaspoons red wine vinegar

Place the dried cranberries in a small bowl and cover them with ¾ cup boiling water. Soak for 20 to 30 minutes, until the cranberries are plump. Drain.

In a small saucepan combine all the ingredients and cook over low heat, stirring frequently so the sugar doesn't burn. The relish is cooked when the apples soften and the onions wilt, about 5 to 7 minutes. Transfer the relish to a small serving bowl and refrigerate for 2 hours. Serve cold.

Makes 1½ cups.

Nora Ephron's Corn Soufflé

Butter to grease pan
2 eggs
2 15-ounce cans creamed corn
1 box Jiffy corn bread mix
3 tablespoons milk
Sour cream (optional)

Preheat oven to 350 degrees.

Butter a 9-x-13-inch baking pan. In a large bowl, lightly beat the eggs. Add the corn, corn bread mix, and milk, and stir until just combined. Turn out into the prepared pan. Top with 6 tablespoon-sized dollops of sour cream, if desired. Bake for 45 minutes, until firm and golden.

Serves 6 to 8.

Damian's Bananas Foster

4 tablespoons unsalted butter (½ stick)

3 bananas or ripe yellow plantains (not the green ones!), peeled and
cut into 1-inch pieces

½ cup packed light brown sugar

¾ cup dark rum

1½ pints vanilla ice cream

Melt the butter in a skillet over medium heat. Add the bananas or plantains and sauté until they begin to brown, about 3 minutes. Sprinkle with the sugar and cook until it melts, about another 3 minutes. Remove from the heat and pour the rum into the skillet. Ignite with a match and let the flames die out.

Spoon the ice cream into bowls and top it with bananas. Dig in!

Serves 6.

FRAN LEBOWITZ DINNER

❋

Beluga Caviar
Olga's Borscht
Stuffed Capon
Blue Cheese and Tomato Salad

❋

They say caviar is an acquired taste, but I must have acquired it in a past life, because I loved it the first moment I tasted it in this one. Heather won't touch the stuff. So it was no wonder that she was slightly disappointed one Christmas when I bought her a beautiful Baccarat crystal caviar dish. "Thanks a *lot*, Jock!" she exclaimed. Of course, I was fully aware of how self-serving the gift was, and had bought her other ones to make up for it.

When I'm feeling especially decadent, I whip out this sparkling creation and put on a superb display. I first fill the bottom bowl with crushed ice, then spoon the glistening caviar into the smaller bowl nestled on top. Around the edges I arrange the appropriate accoutrements: chopped hard-boiled eggs, onions, crème fraîche or sour cream, and toasted squares of thinly sliced white bread.

One night we'd invited the writer Fran Lebowitz over for a Russian-inspired dinner. She was late and missed the hors d'oeuvres. She was also very hungry. After her second helping of capon and salad, she spied the remaining few beads of caviar left in the bowl and scooped them out with her finger. Heather caught her doing this and mentioned that we had more caviar in the kitchen. She brought out the tin, which was still half full, and was about to ladle the caviar into the dish when Fran stopped her. The next thing I knew, Fran was sitting on the floor eating straight from the can. I was happy to join her.

Truth be told, the caviar tasted just as good from the tin as it had from the crystal bowl. So don't be intimidated about serving caviar just because you don't have a fancy setup. Remember, it's only fish eggs.

J.S.

Beluga Caviar

1 8-ounce tin of Beluga (or other) caviar
2 hard-boiled eggs, chopped
1 small white onion, chopped
8 pieces thinly sliced white sandwich bread
½ cup crème fraîche or sour cream

Scoop the caviar into a small glass bowl. Fill a large bowl with crushed ice and place the caviar bowl on top. Around the caviar arrange three separate small bowls filled with, respectively, the chopped hard-boiled egg, the chopped onion, and the crème fraîche or sour cream.

Trim the crusts from the bread and toast. Cut each slice into quarters and arrange them on a platter.

To assemble, spoon a small amount of crème fraîche or sour cream on top of a piece of toast, then top with a small scoop of caviar and, if desired, egg and/or onion.

Serves 8.

Olga's Borscht

1 pound beef spareribs
1 large red onion, peeled and diced
4 large celery ribs, chopped
5 large carrots, peeled and chopped
3 large whole beets, peeled
Salt and pepper
4 Idaho potatoes, peeled and cut into ½-inch cubes
1 cup diced red cabbage
1 cup diced green cabbage
1 large zucchini, diced
1 yellow squash, diced
1 medium red bell pepper, diced
4 tablespoons tomato paste
2 teaspoons chopped fresh mint
3 tablespoons chopped fresh dill, plus extra for garnish
Pinch of curry powder
4 garlic cloves, minced
1 cup sour cream

Place the spareribs in a large stockpot and cover them with 10 cups of water. Add the onion, celery, a little less than half the carrots, the beets, and salt and pepper to taste. Bring to a boil then simmer, covered, for 1½ to 2 hours. Check occasionally, and when the beets soften, remove them and set them aside. When the meat is falling off the bones and the liquid is brownish, remove the pot from the heat and strain the stock. Discard the vegetables, and scrape the meat off the bones and set it aside.

Return the strained stock to a simmer and add the potatoes. When they are almost tender, about 20 minutes, add both red and green cabbage as well as the remaining carrots and the zucchini, squash, and red pepper. Meanwhile, chop the cooled beets. When all the vegetables are tender, about another 20 minutes, add the tomato paste (I usually dissolve it in a little hot broth first). Stir in the mint, dill, curry powder, chopped beets, and minced garlic, and adjust the seasonings to taste.

Simmer for 5 minutes, then add the meat. After 5 more minutes, serve garnished with dollops of sour cream and chopped fresh dill.

Serves 8 to 10.

Stuffed Capon

*D*on't be intimidated when you hear the word "capon." What we're really talking about here are male chickens. I like cooking them because they're juicier and more tender than most commercially available chickens.

10 strips bacon, chopped

1 large onion, chopped

5 medium Idaho potatoes, peeled and diced

3 celery stalks, diced

1 tablespoon chopped fresh oregano (or 1 teaspoon dried)

Salt and pepper

1 6-to-7-pound capon, available from the butcher (Ask the butcher for string, as you will need it later.)

1 cup low-sodium or homemade chicken broth

1 cup white wine

Preheat oven to 400 degrees.

Cook the bacon in a large skillet over medium heat until it's almost crispy. Add the onion, potatoes, celery, and oregano. Cover and cook on low heat until the potatoes are tender, stirring occasionally, about 8 minutes. Season with salt and pepper to taste.

Rinse the capon inside and out in cold water and pat it dry with paper towels. Season it generously inside and out with salt and pepper. Stuff the capon with the bacon-vegetable mixture and truss it firmly.

Place the capon breast side up on a rack set in a roasting pan. Pour the broth and wine into the bottom of the pan. Roast for 20 minutes, then turn the capon over for another 25 minutes. Turn it again, back to breast side up, and reduce the heat to 350 degrees. Continue cooking, basting every now and then. If the liquid in the pan dries up, add water.

After 1 more hour check to see if the capon is done by pricking the thigh with a sharp knife. If the juices run clear, remove it from oven and turn off heat. Scoop the stuffing from the cavity into an ovenproof serving bowl, cover it with aluminum foil, and return it to the oven to keep warm until you're ready to serve. Tent the capon with aluminum foil and allow it to rest for 10 minutes.

Serves 8.

Blue Cheese and Tomato Salad

2 pounds ripe tomatoes
8 tablespoons plain yogurt
½ cup crumbled blue cheese
1 tablespoon white wine vinegar or herb vinegar (such as tarragon)
2 to 3 tablespoons chopped fresh chives
Salt and pepper

Slice the tomatoes about ½ inch thick and arrange them on a serving platter.

Place the yogurt, blue cheese, and vinegar in a small bowl, stir with a fork to combine, and add salt and pepper to taste. Pour the dressing over the tomatoes and top with the chopped chives.

Serves 8.

INSTANT APPETIZERS

*I*n New York, where the catering business can be as competitive as Wall Street, chefs vie to see who can make the most ridiculously complicated finger food. There's something deliciously decadent about consuming in a single bite a morsel that would take me an hour to assemble.

As with homemade desserts, fussy hors d'oeuvres usually aren't at the top of our priority list when we're pressed for time. Appetizers that require only assembly, such as Beluga caviar or smoked salmon, are convenient but wildly expensive.

Here are some ideas for quick, less expensive appetizers that have served us well over the years:

> *Assorted salamis, sliced*
>
> *Pâtés or terrines with cornichons*
>
> *Cheese and crackers (see page 131)*
>
> *Herb-marinated olives (If these aren't available in your local market, rinse brine-cured Kalamata olives under water and place in a clean jar along with assorted herbs such as rosemary, minced garlic, and a bay leaf, and cover with olive oil. Marinate in refrigerator at least overnight.)*
>
> *Crudités (carrots, cucumbers, bell peppers, snow peas, blanched cauliflower, blanched broccoli, blanched asparagus, radishes, turnips) and a selection of simple dips*

CHARLES KURALT DINNER

Smoked Salmon with Brown Bread and Honey Mustard
London Broil on Arugula
Extra-Rich Scalloped Potatoes
Cherry Tomato Salad

The first time I met Charles Kuralt and his wife Petie was when Heather invited me to cook a dinner party in their honor. Of course, I agreed—who wouldn't? I'd been a huge fan of Charles Kuralt's since I first saw him on CBS News as a kid.

We served some wonderful cheeses for appetizers, including Reblochon, a somewhat smelly but delicious French export. Heather also splurged and bought some smoked salmon from Zabar's, the Upper West Side mecca for salmon, sturgeon, and whitefish, as well as other gourmet foods and great housewares.

For the main course we barbecued a juicy London broil out on Heather's terrace, which was overflowing with magnificent roses, one of her greatest loves. Steak needs potatoes, and since this was a special occasion, we decided to go all-out-decadent and serve our favorite cheesy scalloped potatoes. After a big tomato salad, Heather brought out assorted tarts, cookies, and cakes she had picked up from her favorite bakeries all over town.

After this dinner party, I would see Charles and Petie every now and then. One year, they were among the guests at my birthday party and gave me one of the best gifts I've ever received. Charles wrote me the following poem, which now hangs framed in my kitchen, in the place of honor above my spice rack.

27? What a shock!
HAPPY BIRTHDAY, DEAR JOCK!
Wear your age light as a feather.
you still have me
and P.
and Heather . . .
And grace and charm
and splendid youth
(and that is just the honest truth).
What a double life enhancer—
Jock, the famous cooking dancer!

CHARLES KURALT
April 16, 1992

Smoked Salmon with Brown Bread and Honey Mustard

1 bunch fresh dill

2 lemons

8 sandwich-sized slices Russian brown bread, or 32 slices of the
    smaller party size (If neither is available at your local market, thinly
    sliced pumpernickel will do.)

¼ cup honey mustard

¾ pound smoked salmon

2 tablespoons capers

Rinse and dry the dill. Cut each lemon into 8 wedges. Trim the crusts from the bread and, if large size, cut into quarters. Spread a thin layer of honey mustard on the bread, then top with a slice of salmon, trimmed and folded to fit, 1 caper, and a sprig of dill. Arrange the open-faced salmon sandwiches decoratively on a platter with lemon wedges.

Serves 8.

London Broil on Arugula

2 tablespoons Dijon mustard

¾ cup olive oil

3 tablespoons soy sauce

Salt and pepper

2 tablespoons chopped fresh rosemary (or 2 teaspoons dried)

2 tablespoons chopped fresh oregano (or 2 teaspoons dried)

1 4-to-4½-pound London broil

2 tablespoons red wine vinegar

2 large bunches arugula, trimmed, washed, and spun dry

To make the marinade, place the mustard, ½ cup of the olive oil, the soy sauce, a generous amount of black pepper, and the rosemary and oregano in a small bowl and stir to combine. Rinse the steak, pat it dry, and lay it in a shallow dish. Pour the marinade over the meat and turn to coat. Cover the dish with plastic wrap and marinate for 2 hours on the countertop or overnight in the refrigerator, turning once halfway through.

Preheat broiler or prepare grill.

Remove the steak from the marinade. Under the broiler or on the grill, cook for 8 to 10 minutes on each side, depending on how well done you like your meat (I like mine still mooing). Transfer the steak to a cutting board and let it rest for 5 minutes. Slice diagonally into thin strips.

To make the vinaigrette, combine the remaining olive oil, the red wine vinegar, and salt and pepper to taste in a small bowl.

Arrange the arugula on a serving platter. Lay the meat decoratively on top and drizzle with vinaigrette.

Serves 8.

Extra-Rich Scalloped Potatoes

We were introduced to these delicious potatoes by our good friend Anne McNally, who is incredibly chic and, considering this recipe, astonishingly svelte.

4 tablespoons unsalted butter (½ stick)
6 medium unpeeled Idaho potatoes
2 cups grated Gruyère cheese
6 garlic cloves, minced
Salt and pepper
1½ cups light cream
⅔ cup grated Parmesan cheese

Preheat oven to 350 degrees.

Grease a 9-x-13-inch casserole dish with 1 tablespoon of butter. Scrub the potatoes and slice them thin, then arrange a third of the potatoes in a single layer on the bottom of the dish. Top with 1 cup of the Gruyère, half the garlic, and salt and pepper to taste. Repeat with another third of the potatoes, the remaining Gruyère and garlic, and salt and pepper. Follow with a layer of the remaining potatoes. Pour the light cream over the casserole, sprinkle with Parmesan, dot with the remaining butter, and add a final shake of salt and pepper, if desired.

Bake for 90 minutes, until the top is golden.

Serves 8.

Cherry Tomato Salad

*T*his is one of the easiest salads I know, but it works only if the tomatoes are really fresh.

2 pounds ripe cherry tomatoes
1 tablespoon kosher salt
Juice of 1 lemon
2 tablespoons olive oil

Halve the tomatoes and place them in a serving bowl. Add the salt, lemon juice, and olive oil. Stir gently to blend (it's fun to use your hands!). Marinate at room temperature for 1 to 2 hours, or longer in the refrigerator.

Serves 8.

III.

On the Road

*I*n the New York City Ballet, we perform two seasons a year at Lincoln Center—a fourteen-week winter season followed by a nine-week spring season—plus a short, three-week stint every July in Saratoga Springs. For about nine weeks every summer we're laid off, unless we go on tour. The rest of the time, we're in rehearsal for our performances.

One of the bonuses of dancing with the Ballet is touring. I've traveled all over the United States, South America, the Far East, and Europe. Back in 1972, during the height of the Cold War, Heather went on an extraordinary goodwill tour to Russia arranged by Mr. Balanchine—for him a triumphant return to his roots.

While part of the fun of visiting different places is sampling the local cuisine, sometimes there's no substitute for a home-cooked meal. In the cities where we spend more than a few days performing, I try to infuse the tour routine with a little taste of home by hosting a couple of meals if I can find a kitchen. Meals cooked on the road, whether in Saratoga Springs or

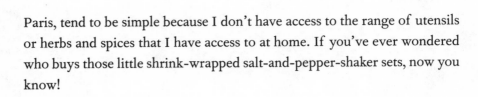

Paris, tend to be simple because I don't have access to the range of utensils or herbs and spices that I have access to at home. If you've ever wondered who buys those little shrink-wrapped salt-and-pepper-shaker sets, now you know!

J.S.

D.C. DINNER

✻

Goat Cheese Toasts
Sausage Pasta
Mesclun Salad with Spanish Sherry Vinaigrette

✻

Pasta has been a lifesaver on tours when we're relegated to nondescript hotel rooms with poorly equipped kitchens. In Washington, D.C., one year, when it seemed we'd eaten at every restaurant within a two-mile radius of the Kennedy Center at least twice, I thought I'd break the monotony by having some of my fellow dancers over for dinner.

We were staying across the street from the infamous Watergate Hotel, which happens to have a huge supermarket on the first floor. I bought all the ingredients there, including the aforementioned salt and pepper shakers. Back in my room, I began cooking the pasta sauce, and everything was going smoothly until I opened the pepper. As I pried up the top, about two tablespoons fell into the sauce. Luckily, my friends had not yet arrived. In a maneuver worthy of Julia Child, I dug out as much pepper as I could and hoped everyone was in the mood for a spicy meal. Luckily, it wound up tasting delicious, which proves how forgiving pasta sauce can be.

J.S.

Goat Cheese Toasts

1 baguette
1 8-ounce log of goat cheese
Freshly ground pepper
Fresh or dried thyme

Preheat broiler.

Saw the baguette into ½-inch slices. Top each slice with a ¼-inch slice of goat cheese. Sprinkle with pepper and thyme to taste.

Broil the toasts until the cheese turns golden, about 5 minutes. Keep a close eye so they don't burn!

Serves 8.

Sausage Pasta

2 tablespoons olive oil

2 pounds sweet and spicy Italian sausage, mixed

2 large onions, diced

10 garlic cloves, minced

2 16-ounce cans of peeled Italian plum tomatoes plus juice

2 tablespoons chopped fresh oregano (or 1 teaspoon dried)

Salt and pepper

2 15-ounce cans of peas, drained

4 tablespoons sour cream

1 cup half-and-half

2 pounds dried pasta (I like to experiment with different shapes, and
   find this sauce goes particularly well with seashells, as they scoop
   it right up.)

Grated Parmesan cheese

Heat the olive oil in a large skillet. Squeeze the sausage out of its casing if the butcher hasn't already done so and add it to the pan, breaking the meat into small pieces with the back of a spoon. Cook for 5 minutes or more, covered, until the sausage begins to brown. Add the onions and garlic and sauté until the onions are translucent and the sausage is fully cooked. Add the tomatoes, oregano, and salt and pepper to taste. Turn the heat to medium-low and cook for about 35 minutes, stirring occasionally. Add the peas, sour cream, and half-and-half, and cook on low for another 10 minutes.

Meanwhile, boil a pot of salted water and cook the pasta according to the directions on the package. Drain and transfer to a large serving bowl. Add the sauce, toss to coat, and serve with grated Parmesan.

Serves 8.

Mesclun Salad with Spanish Sherry Vinaigrette

3 tablespoons Spanish sherry vinegar (La Posada is our favorite
    brand.)
5 tablespoons olive oil
Salt and pepper
10 cups mesclun lettuce

In a salad bowl, combine the vinegar, olive oil, and salt and pepper to taste. Add the lettuce and toss to coat.

Serves 8.

ANNE BASS'S SARATOGA SOIREE

❋

Ulrik's Avocado Soup
Roasted Whole Salmon
Rosemary and Garlic Potatoes

❋

One year in Saratoga Springs, Heather, Ulrik, and I rented a small house just off the Skidmore College campus. We decided to throw a dinner party in honor of our beloved friend Anne Bass, who was visiting from Texas with her daughters, Hyatt and Samantha. Julia Gruen was also up for the weekend, and we invited Bruce Padgett and Peter Martins, which brought the total number of diners to nine. Fortunately, we had enough plates and utensils—not always the case in a rental.

Anne Bass is a great patron of the ballet as well as a renowned hostess with impeccable taste. Although we were nervous, we were also excited at the chance to thank her for the many evenings she had wined and dined us in her beautiful homes. That afternoon, Heather and I went on a stealth mission to collect flowers for the table. The neighborhood was filled with summer gardens, so we helped ourselves. I cut while Heather acted as lookout. We found out crime doesn't pay. Just before the guests arrived at eight, we discovered that day lilies are aptly named! Fortunately, we had enough wildflowers to camouflage the wilted loot.

The kitchen was small and not very well stocked. While Heather and I prepared the salmon and vegetables, Ulrik worked on the soup. We knew he was trying to be helpful, but he used so much of the scarce counter space that he drove us crazy. Calmness prevailed, however, and the end product was delicious and received many accolades from our guests.

J.S.

Ulrik's Avocado Soup

8 large ripe avocados
5 cups plain low-fat yogurt
5 cups low-sodium or homemade chicken broth
10 tablespoons lemon juice
Salt and pepper
¾ teaspoon cayenne pepper
Chopped fresh cilantro, basil, or chives for garnish

In a food processor or blender, puree seven of the avocados with the yogurt, chicken broth, lemon juice, salt, and peppers. Chill for at least 3 hours in the refrigerator.

Distribute the soup among 8 bowls. Garnish with the remaining avocado, thinly sliced, and the chopped herbs.

Serves 8.

Roasted Whole Salmon

Roasting is the best way to retain the moisture and tenderness of salmon. It also takes almost no time to prepare and cook. The downside is that your oven will be a mess and smell of fish, so be prepared for a morning-after date with the Easy-Off.

> 1 whole 4-pound salmon (If it's too big for your roasting pan, have the head and tail cut off.)
> 1 lemon
> 3 tablespoons olive oil
> 1 tablespoon kosher salt
> 1 tablespoon cracked black pepper

Preheat oven to 500 degrees.

Rinse the salmon thoroughly under cold water and pat it dry. Place the salmon in a large roasting pan and make three diagonal slits in each side, cutting almost through to the bone. Squeeze the lemon all over the fish, including in the slits. Rub the olive oil and salt and pepper over the outside.

Place the fish in the oven and roast for 20 minutes. Remove and let it stand 10 minutes before slicing. The skin should peel back easily; be careful to avoid bones.

Serves 8 to 10.

Rosemary and Garlic Potatoes

12 medium red potatoes, unpeeled and cut into quarters
5 tablespoons olive oil
8 garlic cloves, minced
3 tablespoons chopped fresh rosemary (or 3 teaspoons dried)
Salt and pepper

Preheat oven to 375 degrees.

Combine all the ingredients in a roasting pan or casserole dish. Bake for approximately 1 hour, stirring occasionally, until golden brown. (This dish may be made an hour in advance and reheated while the salmon is resting.)

Serves 8.

Kitchen Checklist

One of the fun things about setting up a new house is stocking the kitchen. When we bought our house in Connecticut, we all contributed whatever extra appliances and utensils we had or didn't use in our much smaller city kitchens. Unfortunately, we ended up with three coffee grinders and no sharp knives—and of course, you'd only notice you were missing, say, a whisk when you were halfway through a recipe that required it. We all agreed it would have been great to have had a checklist to take inventory of what we already had and what we needed. One lesson we learned the hard way—it pays to invest in quality pots and pans. For all future new homeowners, here is our complete list:

12-inch skillet	colander	scissors
stockpot	steamer	string
1-quart saucepan	4-sided grater	molded plastic juicer
roasting pan	vegetable peeler	carving fork
Pyrex casserole	garlic press	tongs
toaster oven	hand-held blender	skewers
can opener	rolling pin	pastry brush
2-cup measuring cup	blender	melon scooper
8-inch chopping knife	pie plate	ice cream scooper
paring knife	timer	baster
serrated knife	roasting rack	rubber spatula
knife steel	food processor	corkscrew
ladle	hand-held mixer	barbecue brush
measuring spoons	potato masher	tart pan
wooden spoon	meat thermometer	baking sheet
spatula	oven mitts	cake pans
slotted spoon	cutting board	loaf pan
whisk	nested mixing bowls	muffin pan

DESTINY, PALOMINO, LITTLE BEAR, SKYE, BLUE, AND EVEN FRED AND Q'S TRIPLE-PASTA PARTY

❁

Linguine with Pesto Sauce
Penne with Uncooked Tomato-Basil Sauce
Bow Ties with Gorgonzola Sauce
Tricolor Salad

❁

*I*t's funny how you meet the people who change your life. In 1987, Jock and I began spending our day off from the New York City Ballet in the kitchen of God's Love We Deliver, an organization that provides meals for homebound people with AIDS. Slicing and dicing carrots, potatoes, and broccoli, or washing endless piles of lasagna pans, we worked alongside many wonderful volunteers. The incredibly warm and funny Frances Murdoch was one of them.

Fran-tic (as we call her) asked us to do a benefit performance for the Lake Placid Center for the Arts in July during our Saratoga season. A carload of us left Saratoga early on Sunday morning, exhausted from a long week of dancing, so we were delighted to be the guests of Fran's wonderful friends, the Birds. Their compound on Upper St. Regis Lake was beautiful and we spent a long day swimming, boating, and relaxing. At dusk, we all piled into boats and puttered over to the Adirondack "camp" of the great photographer Bruce Weber and his girlfriend, Nan Bush. They had put on an Italian feast of three different pastas, a huge salad, and a selection of succulent summer fruit pies. We ate and drank long into the night. This memorable evening became the highlight of our trip, which turned into a much-anticipated annual event. As my retirement from dancing approached, I often thought of how much I'd miss these magical evenings.

As fate would have it, Graydon Carter, editor in chief of *Vanity Fair*, offered me an unexpected door to the future. As a contributing editor, I now attend arts, culture, and book meetings and submit story ideas for the magazine. My first idea for the magazine was, naturally, my greatest passion, the New York City Ballet. I suggested a story on the male stars at the company and Graydon was mildly interested, but when I suggested Bruce Weber as the perfect photographer for the story, he gave an enthusiastic go-ahead. I had long been awed by Bruce's sensitive genius and was excited at the opportunity to work with him. I called him and he readily agreed to shoot the story, and I felt charmed when I found myself once again enjoying July on the lake.

Bruce and I have traveled quite a bit lately—from the Adirondacks to Cape Kennedy, from Miami to Gstaad, covering subjects from Buzz Aldrin to Allegra Kent, and Dave Brubeck to Balthus. Graydon's trust in me has allowed me to take the first steps away from my ballet career, and Bruce's unerring eye has shown me a whole new world.

Bruce, Nan, and I share an overwhelming love of our golden retrievers and when we've been on the road too long, we find ourselves talking about them too much. Since a night in the Adirondacks would not be complete without their warm and silly presence, Nan and Bruce's Italian feast menu is dedicated to all our beloved dogs.

H.W.

Linguine with Pesto Sauce

2 cups firmly packed fresh basil, washed and dried
4 garlic cloves, peeled
¼ cup toasted pine nuts
⅓ cup olive oil
½ cup grated Parmesan cheese
Salt and pepper
1 pound linguine

In a food processor, grind the basil, garlic, and pine nuts to a paste. With the machine running, add the olive oil in a steady stream until well incorporated. Add the Parmesan cheese and process to combine. Mix in salt and pepper to taste.

Cook the pasta according to the package directions. Drain and transfer to a serving bowl. Toss with the pesto sauce.

Serves 4.

Penne with Uncooked Tomato-Basil Sauce

5 large very ripe summer tomatoes, chopped

3 garlic cloves, minced

1 small red onion, diced

1 tablespoon chopped fresh oregano

8 ounces fresh unsalted mozzarella cheese, diced

¼ cup chopped fresh basil

Salt and pepper

¼ cup olive oil

½ cup grated Parmesan cheese

1 pound penne

In a bowl combine the tomatoes, garlic, onion, oregano, mozzarella, and basil. Add salt and pepper to taste. Stir in the olive oil.

Cook the pasta according to the package directions. Drain and transfer to a serving bowl. Add the sauce and ¼ cup of the Parmesan cheese and toss to coat.

Serve, passing the remaining ¼ cup of Parmesan on the side.

Serves 4.

Bow Ties with Gorgonzola Sauce

8 tablespoons (1 stick) unsalted butter
2 garlic cloves, pressed
½ pound Gorgonzola cheese, cut into small pieces
1 cup half-and-half
1½ teaspoons chopped fresh thyme (or ½ teaspoon dried)
1 pound bow ties
½ cup grated Parmesan cheese
Salt and pepper

In a saucepan over medium heat, melt the butter and add the garlic. Cook for 2 minutes, until the garlic softens. Add the Gorgonzola, half-and-half, and thyme and cook over a low flame until the cheese melts and the sauce thickens.

Cook the bow ties according to the package directions. Transfer to a serving bowl. Add the sauce and the Parmesan and toss to coat. Salt and pepper to taste.

Serves 4.

Tricolor Salad

3 garlic cloves, crushed
½ cup olive oil
1 tablespoon Dijon mustard
2 tablespoons red wine vinegar
Salt and pepper
1 medium head radicchio
1 large endive
2 medium bunches arugula, trimmed, washed, and dried

In a small bowl combine the garlic, olive oil, mustard, vinegar, and salt and pepper to taste.

With a serrated knife, cut the radicchio into ¼-inch shreds. With a straight knife, cut the endive into ¼-inch slices. Place the endive and radicchio in a salad bowl with the arugula. Add the dressing and toss to coat.

Serves 8.

A DINNER CELEBRATING JOHN BASS

❄

Fillet of Beef
Horseradish Sauce
Crispy Potato Pancake

❄

*I*t was the strangest thing. One night a bunch of us were having dinner at Jane and John Gruen's house. John Bass walked in with his right eye completely closed. He planned to see the doctor about it the next day, but felt fine otherwise. Over the next couple of weeks he had a zillion tests. The doctors decided he had a rare form of cancer and admitted him to the hospital for chemotherapy.

When I went to visit John with Heather and Ulrik, there was a sign on his door saying, "Caution: Potential Immunodeficiency Syndrome"—this was a couple of years before the HIV test was developed, in the very early stage of the AIDS epidemic. We walked into the room and were shocked to find John sitting in bed, frighteningly gaunt and completely bald. It had only been two or three weeks since the dinner. He lived for another year like that, in and out of the hospital, undergoing rounds and rounds of chemotherapy. That fall, in Washington, we got a call saying John had died.

Heather and I were dancing in every performance that weekend—I even had a couple of premieres—so only Ulrik could go back to New York to attend the funeral. After the matinee was over on Sunday afternoon, I finally allowed the news to sink in. I went directly to the grocery store, bought a whole bunch of ingredients, hauled them back to our hotel, and started cooking. The methodical nature of the chopping and preparing helped keep my mind off of how distraught I was feeling.

Ulrik returned and soon our suite was filled with people. Everybody was crying at first, but then we started drinking and eating and laughing and telling our favorite stories about John. Sharing a meal helped ease our pain and reminded us that there was still joy and pleasure and beauty in this world, even though John was no longer with us.

J.S.

Fillet of Beef

4 tablespoons Dijon mustard

1 small can green peppercorns

2 teaspoons olive oil

Freshly ground pepper

3 pounds fillet of beef (Ask the butcher for string if the meat is not
tied already.)

Horseradish Sauce (page 99)

Preheat oven to 350 degrees.

In a small bowl mix the mustard, peppercorns, olive oil, and a generous
amount of pepper. Try to smash the peppercorns as well as you can.

Rinse the fillet in cold water and pat it dry with paper towels. If the
butcher hasn't already done so, roll the meat into a log and tie it tightly with
string. Smear the marinade all over the meat and place it in a roasting pan.
Put the pan in the oven and bake 35 minutes for rare, longer for more well
done.

Remove the fillet from the oven and let it stand for 10 minutes. Slice and
serve with Horseradish Sauce.

Serves 6.

Horseradish Sauce

*T*his sauce is delicious on fish as well as steak.

 1 cup sour cream
 4 tablespoons bottled horseradish
 1 tablespoon mustard
 1 tablespoon olive oil
 ½ teaspoon white wine vinegar
 Salt and pepper

Combine all of the ingredients. Season to taste and chill.

 Serves 6.

Crispy Potato Pancake

4 unpeeled Idaho potatoes, washed and sliced thin
4 tablespoons (½ stick) unsalted butter, softened
Salt and pepper

Preheat oven to 400 degrees.

Grease the bottom of a 10-inch ovenproof (cast-iron or enameled iron, such as Le Creuset) skillet. Arrange a quarter of the potato slices in a layer on the bottom. Dot with butter, generously salt and pepper, and top with a second layer of potatoes, followed by butter and seasonings. Combine until all of the ingredients are used. Place the skillet in the oven and bake for about 1 hour and 15 minutes, until the top is golden brown. Slide onto a serving plate.

Serves 6.

IV.

Holidays at Home

Holidays and special occasions are important to everyone. Thanksgiving, Christmas, New Year's, and birthdays are more than just opportunities to gather loved ones, they are reliable landmarks in our ever-changing lives.

When we first began spending holidays together, hauling our home-roasted turkey with all the fixings to friends' houses in upstate New York or southern Connecticut, we unconsciously became one another's families. When we began looking, with Damian, for a home of our own, we followed our friends to Washington, Connecticut, which we adore for its beauty and privacy. Of course, our idea of privacy isn't everyone's—at last count, five of our friends and siblings, a godfather, a niece, a boss, and countless acquaintances live within a ten-mile radius. We adhere to no strict rules—sometimes we see each other a lot and sometimes we bury ourselves in chores or a good book. Holidays, however, are the exception—everybody comes to our house and we

prepare a great feast. We cherish the family of friends we've created for ourselves over all these years. After nearly a lifetime of dancing "The Nutcracker" every Christmas, it's nice to start a new tradition of our own.

H. and J.

THANKSGIVING DINNER

✱

Butternut Squash Soup
Turkey with Sage-and-Sausage Stuffing and Gravy
Damian's Cranberry Sauce
Honeyed Yams
Asparagus with Lemon Vinaigrette
Stilton, Bacon, and Mesclun Salad
Apple-Cheddar Crumble
Pumpkin Pie

✱

Thanksgiving is hands down my favorite holiday. If you think about it, it's a day entirely dedicated to celebrating food—from the corn the Native Americans shared with the Pilgrims to the turkey that graces our Thanksgiving table. We do all our shopping in advance in the city, then drive up to the country after the performance on Wednesday night. Thursday is a marathon cookfest, with people trickling in all day long. Heather's sister Jennifer and her husband Mitch always come (now, with their adorable baby daughter, Savannah), as do my parents, who drive down from Rhode Island, where they now live. And it wouldn't be Thanksgiving without Damian's godfather, Abdo, who recently moved to the area. Any friends without a place to go are always welcome—we usually end up with more than a dozen people. Though we spend hours at the table, there are always plenty of leftovers to snack on for the rest of the weekend.

J.S.

Butternut Squash Soup

1 tablespoon spicy flavored oil (Heather likes to use garlic oil or
    jalapeño oil.)
2 1-pound butternut squash, halved and seeded
2 tablespoons olive oil or unsalted butter
1 medium onion, diced
3 large carrots, peeled and diced
6 cups low-sodium or homemade chicken broth
1 tablespoon honey
Salt and pepper

Preheat oven to 400 degrees.

Drizzle the spicy oil over the cut squash halves and place them cut side up on a baking sheet. Bake for 45 minutes, until soft. When they're cool enough to handle, scoop out the insides of the squash with a spoon and place in a bowl.

Heat the olive oil or butter in a stockpot. Sauté the onions until translucent, then add the carrots and squash and cook for another 10 minutes. Add the broth and bring to a boil. Reduce the heat, cover, and simmer until the carrots are cooked, about 15 minutes. Puree the soup in a blender or food processor, or with a hand-held blender, then return it to the pot and reheat. Stir in the honey and salt and pepper to taste.

Serves 6 to 8.

Turkey with Sage-and-Sausage Stuffing and Gravy

STUFFING

    1 tablespoon olive oil

    1 large onion, diced

    3 pounds sweet sausage

    5 celery stalks, diced

    3 medium carrots, diced

    4 fresh sage leaves, chopped (or 1½ tablespoons dried)

    Salt and pepper

    2 cups bread crumbs or 3 cups cubed stale French or Italian bread

Heat the olive oil in a large skillet. Sauté the onion for 5 minutes. Add the sausage—if not ground, squeeze it from its casing into the pan and break it up with the back of a spoon—and cook until it begins to brown. Add the celery, carrots, sage, and salt and pepper to taste. Sauté until the sausage is thoroughly cooked. Stir in the bread crumbs or bread and remove from the heat.

TURKEY

    1 20-pound turkey at room temperature, and string for trussing

    Salt and pepper

    3 medium onions, sliced

    10 garlic cloves, peeled

    Handful of sprigs of fresh thyme and/or rosemary

    At least ½ cup port wine

Preheat oven to 350 degrees.

Remove the innards, gizzards, and all that good stuff from the turkey. Wash it inside and out in cold water and pat dry. Salt and pepper liberally, both inside and out. Spoon the stuffing into the cavity until it's completely full (leftover stuffing may be baked in a dish alongside the bird, covered with aluminum foil). Place a small piece of aluminum foil in the opening so

the stuffing doesn't fall out and tie the legs together. Place the turkey in a roasting pan breast side down. Scatter the onion, garlic, herbs, and, if desired, innards around the bird. Add ½ cup water to the pan and pour the port over the turkey.

Place the turkey in the oven and roast for 1 hour, basting every 10 to 15 minutes. Turn the turkey breast side up and cook for approximately 3 more hours, continuing to baste. If the skin threatens to burn, tent with aluminum foil. The turkey is cooked when juices from a pierced thigh run clear.

Remove the turkey from the oven and reduce the temperature to 250 degrees. Transfer the turkey to a serving platter. Immediately scoop the stuffing into a casserole dish, cover with aluminum foil, and return to oven. Tent the turkey with aluminum foil to keep it warm.

GRAVY
Turkey drippings
3 tablespoons flour
2½ cups low-sodium or homemade chicken broth
Salt and pepper

Discard the onions, garlic, and herbs from the juice in the roasting pan, then place the pan over two burners on the stove. Bring to a simmer, then quickly whisk in the flour. Still whisking, gradually add the chicken broth. When a gravylike consistency is reached, add salt and pepper to taste.

Serves 20, with leftovers.

Damian's Cranberry Sauce

1 12-ounce bag fresh cranberries
½ cup sugar
Grated zest and juice of 1 orange
1 tablespoon cognac

Place the cranberries and ¾ cup water in a large saucepan and bring to a boil. Add the sugar and simmer for 10 to 15 minutes, until the cranberry skins pop and the sugar dissolves. Skim off any white foam. Remove from the heat and stir in the orange zest and juice and the cognac. Chill in the refrigerator until ready to serve.

Serves 8.

Honeyed Yams

Once I got into a big argument with someone about sweet potatoes and yams. He said that what I called yams were actually sweet potatoes, and that real yams were much bigger. I said that I'd grown up calling yams yams and I wasn't about to change. Nobody has ever had a problem understanding what I'm referring to—the torpedo-shaped potatoes with brown skin and orange insides—and nobody has ever had a problem eating them when I prepare them according to this recipe.

4 large yams (or sweet potatoes, if it makes you happy)
4 tablespoons (½ stick) unsalted butter, cut into small pieces
½ cup honey
⅓ cup half-and-half
Salt and pepper

Preheat oven to 400 degrees.

Bake the yams for 1 hour. Cool, cut in half, and scoop the insides into a pan. Add the butter, honey, and half-and-half. Over medium heat, mash all of the ingredients with a potato masher. Add salt and pepper to taste.

Serves 6.

Asparagus with Lemon Vinaigrette

3 tablespoons olive oil
Juice of 1½ lemons
1 teaspoon Dijon mustard
½ teaspoon cumin
2 pounds asparagus, washed and trimmed
1 tablespoon chopped fresh tarragon

In a small bowl, mix the olive oil, lemon juice, mustard, and cumin, and chill.

Steam the asparagus for about 5 minutes, until tender but still a little crunchy. Drain in a colander and run under cold water to stop cooking.

Arrange the asparagus on a serving plate. Drizzle with the vinaigrette and sprinkle with the tarragon.

Serves 6 to 8.

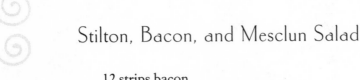

Stilton, Bacon, and Mesclun Salad

12 strips bacon
8 cups mesclun lettuce
12 cherry tomatoes, halved
½ cup crumbled Stilton cheese
5 tablespoons olive oil
2 garlic cloves, minced
2 tablespoons red wine vinegar
1½ teaspoons Dijon mustard
Salt and pepper

Cook the bacon in a skillet until crispy. Remove and drain on paper towels. When it's cool, crumble and set aside.

Place the lettuce and tomatoes in large salad bowl. Sprinkle the cheese on top.

In a small bowl combine the olive oil, garlic, vinegar, mustard, and salt and pepper to taste. Drizzle the vinaigrette over the salad and toss to coat.

Serves 6 to 8.

Apple-Cheddar Crumble

2 pounds mixed tart apples (McIntosh, Granny Smith), peeled, cored,
  and sliced
1 cup firmly packed light brown sugar
2 teaspoons ground cinnamon
1 teaspoon ground nutmeg
½ teaspoon ground cardamom
⅔ cups flour
1½ cups (6 ounces) shredded Cheddar cheese—fresh, not from a bag!
4 tablespoons (½ stick) chilled unsalted butter, cut into pieces
Fresh whipped cream or ice cream

Preheat oven to 400 degrees.

In a 3-quart casserole toss the apples with ⅔ cup of brown sugar and the
cinnamon, nutmeg, and cardamom. In a small bowl combine the remaining
sugar, the flour, and the cheese. Add the butter and work in with your fin-
gers until the mixture resembles coarse crumbs. Sprinkle the topping over
the apples.

Bake for 35 to 40 minutes, until the apples are tender and juicy and the
topping is golden. Serve with fresh whipped cream or vanilla ice cream as an
accompaniment.

Serves 10 to 12.

Pumpkin Pie

CRUST

    ¾ cup vegetable shortening
    1 tablespoon milk
    ¼ teaspoon salt
    2 cups flour

In a bowl stir together the shortening and ¼ cup boiling water until smooth. Add the milk and salt and stir to combine.

Place the flour in the bowl of a food processor. Add the shortening mixture and process until smooth. Form into a ball, wrap in waxed paper, then refrigerate for 1 hour.

FILLING

    3 eggs
    ⅓ cup sugar
    ⅓ cup brown sugar
    2 cups canned pureed pumpkin
    1½ teaspoons ground cinnamon
    ½ teaspoon ground cloves
    ½ teaspoon ground allspice
    ¼ teaspoon ground cardamom
    1½ cups heavy cream

Combine the eggs and both sugars in a large bowl and beat until light and fluffy. Beat in the pumpkin puree and spices, followed by the cream.

1½ tablespoons chopped crystallized ginger

Preheat oven to 425 degrees.

Roll the dough out on a floured surface and transfer it to a 9-inch pie pan. Trim and crimp the edges. Pour in the filling.

Bake for 10 minutes, then reduce the heat to 300 degrees and bake for another 45 minutes, until the filling is firm. Remove from the oven and sprinkle with the crystallized ginger. Cool the pie completely before cutting.

Serves 8.

CHRISTMAS FEAST

❄

Prime Rib au Jus
Yorkshire Pudding
Steamed Broccoli with Lemon Vinaigrette
Carrots with Shallots and Honey
Chris's Mince Tarts
Pecan Pie

❄

We usually spend Christmas in Connecticut with just our "immediate" family. We drive up to the house on the twenty-third after "The Nutcracker" and cook all day on the twenty-fourth, filling the house with the delicious aromas of Christmas. I love to decorate the house and lawn with lights—if I'm not restrained, it winds up looking like the famed New York restaurant Tavern on the Green!

Partly because of the many European influences on our lives and partly because we—like many children—can't wait, we open our gifts on Christmas Eve after a glorious dinner.

H.W.

Prime Rib au Jus

4 pounds prime rib
1 cup dry red wine
8 turns of pepper mill
¼ cup steak sauce (I use sauce from the Brooklyn steak house Peter Luger.)
¼ cup balsamic vinegar
2 tablespoons Dijon mustard
3 garlic cloves, minced

Rinse the meat under cold water and pat it dry with paper towels. Place it in a shallow dish.

In a small bowl combine the red wine, pepper, steak sauce, vinegar, mustard, and garlic and pour the marinade over the prime rib. Turn the meat to coat both sides, cover with plastic wrap, and refrigerate for 2 to 4 hours.

Preheat oven to 500 degrees.

Transfer the prime rib to a roasting pan. Place it in the oven and roast for 15 minutes. Reduce the heat to 325 degrees and continue cooking. After about an hour check for doneness—a meat thermometer placed in the thickest part of the meat away from the bone should read 130 degrees for medium rare.

Remove the roast from the oven and tent with aluminum foil. Let the meat rest for 10 to 15 minutes before slicing. Pass the meat juice separately.

Serves 8 to 10.

Yorkshire Pudding

2 cups flour
Salt and pepper
2 large eggs
¾ cup milk
1½ tablespoons vegetable oil

Preheat oven to 425 degrees.

Sift the flour and a pinch of salt and pepper into a mixing bowl. Make a well in the center of the flour. Break the eggs into the well and beat them in with a hand-held mixer. Gradually incorporate the milk and ½ cup water until the batter is smooth. Refrigerate for 30 minutes.

Grease a casserole dish with the vegetable oil, and heat it, empty, for 5 minutes in the oven. Place the batter in the dish and cook for 35 to 45 minutes. When done, the pudding should be puffy, golden brown, and crisp on top. Serve immediately.

Serves 8.

Steamed Broccoli with Lemon Vinaigrette

6 cups broccoli florets
4 tablespoons olive oil
Juice of 1½ lemons
1 tablespoon fresh tarragon, or 1 teaspoon dried
Salt and pepper

Preheat oven to 350 degrees.

Steam the broccoli florets until tender but still slightly crunchy.

Place olive oil, lemon juice, and tarragon in the bottom of a serving bowl. Lightly whisk. Add salt and pepper to taste. Add broccoli and toss gently.

Serves 6.

Carrots with Shallots and Honey

4 tablespoons unsalted butter (¼ stick)
6 cups baby carrots
4 shallots, minced
4 tablespoons honey
Salt and pepper

Melt the butter in a medium saucepan. Add the carrots, shallots, and honey. Cover and cook over medium heat, stirring occasionally, for about 15 minutes, until the carrots are cooked but still slightly crunchy. Add salt and pepper to taste.

Serves 6 to 8.

Chris's Mince Tarts

*C*hris makes these traditional dried-fruit pies every year, based on his mom's recipe.

CRUST

> 2 cups flour
> 8 tablespoons (1 stick) unsalted butter, chilled and cut into pieces
> 4 tablespoons vegetable shortening or lard, chilled
> Grated zest and juice of 1 orange
> 3 tablespoons ice water

Place 1¾ cups flour, the butter, and the vegetable shortening or lard in the bowl of a food processor fitted with a metal blade. Process just until the mixture resembles coarse crumbs, about 10 seconds. Add the orange zest and juice and pulse to mix. If necessary, add the water little by little, slowly pulsing after each addition, until the pastry begins to hold together (you may not need all 3 tablespoons of water, but you certainly won't need more).

The second the dough forms a ball, stop processing and turn it out onto waxed paper. Mold it into a biscuit shape. If the dough is excessively sticky, incorporate some of the remaining flour. Wrap it in waxed paper and refrigerate for at least 30 minutes.

ASSEMBLY

> 6 cups mincemeat (This is available at specialty shops; be sure to ask
>   for vegetarian mincemeat.)
> 1 egg yolk
> 3 ounces ground almonds
> 6 tablespoons sugar

Preheat oven to 400 degrees.

Remove the dough from the refrigerator and roll it out on a generously floured surface. Cut it into rounds and press a round into each of 12 muffin cups. Fill each crust with ½ cup of the mincemeat.

Lightly beat the egg yolk and fold in the ground almonds and sugar. Top each pie with a spoonful of this mixture. Bake for about 30 minutes, until the tops are golden brown. Cool completely before turning out pies.

Serves 12.

Pecan Pie

CRUST
    ¾ cup vegetable shortening
    1 tablespoon milk
    ¼ teaspoon salt
    2 cups flour

In a bowl stir together the shortening and ¼ cup boiling water until smooth. Add the milk and salt and stir to combine.

Place the flour in the bowl of a food processor. Add the shortening mixture and process until smooth. Form the dough into a ball, wrap it in waxed paper, then refrigerate for 1 hour.

FILLING
    4 eggs
    1 cup dark brown sugar
    ¾ cup light corn syrup
    4 tablespoons (½ stick) unsalted butter, melted
    1 teaspoon vanilla extract

In a large bowl, beat the eggs well. Stir in the brown sugar, corn syrup, melted butter, and vanilla and mix well.

ASSEMBLY
    2 cups shelled pecans, chopped
    ½ cup shelled pecan halves

Preheat oven to 425 degrees.

Roll the dough out on a floured surface. Transfer it to a 9-inch pie plate and trim and crimp the edges. Sprinkle the chopped pecans in the bottom of the crust. Pour the filling over the chopped pecans. Arrange pecan halves over the top of the pie for decoration.

Bake the pie for 15 minutes in the middle of the oven. Reduce the temperature to 350 and bake for another 15 to 20 minutes, until just set—do not overbake!

Serves 8.

NEW YEAR'S EVE PARTY

❋

Caesar Salad
Poached Salmon with Dill Hollandaise Sauce
Stuffed Goose
Morning-After Fried Potatoes

❋

Back when Ulrik and I were living in our spatially challenged Chelsea apartment, we hosted a New Year's Eve party for about forty people. We both cooked—he made a wonderful salmon and a goose, while I took care of all the appetizers and the Caesar salad. In a frenzy of efficiency, I made the salad at four in the afternoon. By the time the guests began to arrive, around nine, it was a disgusting soggy mess. Incredibly, people still ate it. That night I learned a crucial culinary strategy: If you want to disguise a failed dish, ply your guests with lots of champagne!

J.S.

Caesar Salad

3 cups diced French bread
2 egg yolks
2 tablespoons lemon juice
3 garlic cloves, mashed
4 anchovies
Salt and pepper
½ cup grated Parmesan cheese
⅓ cup olive oil
1 head romaine lettuce, washed and sliced into 1½-inch ribbons

To make delicious croutons, simply brown the bread cubes in a dry skillet over medium heat. Set aside.

Combine the egg yolks, lemon juice, garlic, and anchovies, salt and pepper to taste, and 2 tablespoons of the Parmesan cheese in the bottom of a big salad bowl. While continuously whisking, add the olive oil in a stream. Add the lettuce and remaining Parmesan cheese. Toss to coat and top with the croutons.

Serves 6 to 8.

Poached Salmon with Dill Hollandaise Sauce

SAUCE

  3 egg yolks
  3 tablespoons fresh lemon juice
  12 tablespoons (1½ sticks) unsalted butter, melted
  3 tablespoons chopped fresh dill
  Salt and pepper

In a heavy saucepan or the top of a double boiler, whisk together the egg yolks and lemon juice over medium heat until the sauce begins to thicken (about 5 minutes). Remove the pan from the heat and gradually add the melted butter, whisking constantly. Stir in the dill and salt and pepper to taste.

FISH

  1 bottle white wine
  1 large carrot, peeled and cut into sticks
  1 large stalk celery, cut into sticks
  1 medium onion, cut into eighths
  12 black peppercorns
  1 teaspoon salt
  1 bay leaf
  4 sprigs fresh parsley
  1 4-to-5-pound salmon, head and tail left on (if you can fit it into your
      poacher—otherwise have the salesperson remove them)

Place a fish poacher (or large roasting pan with a lid) over 2 burners on the stove. Add the wine, 3 cups of water, carrot, celery, onion, peppercorns, salt, bay leaf, and parsley. Bring to a boil, then cover and simmer for 15 minutes to blend the flavors.

Meanwhile, rinse the salmon, inside and out, in cold water and pat it dry with paper towels. When the broth is cooked, transfer the salmon to the

poacher. Add more water if necessary, to cover the fish completely. Cover the poacher and simmer for 25 minutes. Be extremely careful transferring the fish to a serving platter, as it is extremely slippery and burning hot.

The salmon may be served hot, cold, or at room temperature with the Dill Hollandaise Sauce.

Serves 20 buffet style, or 8 to 10 as a main course.

Stuffed Goose

*U*lrik's mother, Ruth, is very particular about her geese. According to Ruth, the geese available in the United States are much fattier than those in Denmark, which are similar to Canadian geese. She says it's imperative to cook the goose on a rack so it's not sitting in drippings and to siphon off the fat at regular intervals. The fat may be saved in the refrigerator and used as a substitute for oil or butter in a variety of dishes, such as the Morning-After Fried Potatoes that follow.

1 10-pound goose, and string for trussing
Salt and pepper
2 cups pitted prunes
3 cups apples, peeled, cored, and sliced

Preheat oven to 475 degrees.

Rinse the goose in cold water and pat it dry with paper towels. Salt and pepper liberally, both inside and out. Stuff the bird with the prunes and apples, then truss it tightly.

Place the goose on a rack mounted in a roasting pan, breast side down, and place it in the oven. After 30 minutes, turn the goose over and siphon off all but ¼ inch of liquid from the pan. Cook for another hour, siphoning off fat every 20 minutes. The goose is cooked when juices from a pricked thigh run clear.

Remove the goose from the oven. Let it rest 10 minutes before carving.

Serves 15 buffet style, or 6 as main course.

Morning-After Fried Potatoes

One happy consequence of our obese American geese is that the left-over fat can be used the next day to make the world's most decadent fried potatoes.

  6 medium Idaho potatoes, peeled
  3 tablespoons goose fat
  Salt and pepper

Bring a large pot of water to a boil, then drop in the potatoes. Boil them until they're soft when pricked with a fork, about 15 minutes. Drain and slice into ¼-inch-thick rounds.

Heat the goose fat in a large skillet. Add the potatoes and sauté until crisp and brown. Add salt and pepper to taste.

Serves 6 to 8.

INDISPENSABLE CHEESES!

As you've probably noticed by now, Jock and I eat a lot of cheese. I'd like to think it's because we work out so much, but we're probably just dairy junkies.

We eat cheese in a variety of ways: on crackers for hors d'oeuvres, as garnishes for salads, melted on toast, grated on pastas, or just by the slice on sandwiches. We eat all kinds of cheese: hard, soft, strong, mild, French, Greek, American, Italian. I live around the corner from Fairway, a market with a great cheese selection, and I frequently stop by the cheese counter to try something new. I love exotic cheeses, but here is a list of the tried-and-true, some of which we always have on hand.

Parmigiano Reggiano

Vermont Cheddar

English Stilton blue cheese

Swiss Emmentaler

Brie

Reblochon

Saga Blue

Mozzarella

Gruyère

Fresh goat cheese

Greek feta

Monterey Jack

Gorgonzola

BIG BIRTHDAY BASH

❃

Garlic Bread

Lasagna

Special-Occasion German Chocolate Cake

❃

Jock's thirtieth birthday came several months after my retirement from the New York City Ballet. It was the first busy rehearsal season that I was not involved in, and since Jock and Damian were dancing eight hours a day, I realized I was going to have to throw Jock's party on my own. For me, this was not as easy as it sounds. Jock has the most eclectic group of friends—I knew that the dancers would be famished from their long day of rehearsal, some of our more social friends would have nibbled on Glorious Foods at a cocktail party, and the downtown artists would be arriving late, as usual. I would have to be ready for anywhere from thirty to fifty people. The most practical thing was, obviously, a buffet.

For dessert, I used a wonderful German chocolate cake recipe that Michael James gave us a long time ago and that I have continued to play with over the years—it's one of our favorites. It needed to be made a day in advance so it could "ripen." I bought three delicious loaves of bread to warm at different times and made three separate pans of lasagna, to be cooked at various points throughout the evening. A large simple salad completed the meal and left me free to spend most of the evening with Jock.

H. W.

Garlic Bread

8 tablespoons (1 stick) unsalted butter, softened
5 garlic cloves, minced
1 loaf French or Italian bread

Preheat the broiler.

Combine the butter and garlic in a bowl. Slice the loaf in half length-wise. Smear the cut sides with the garlic-butter mixture. Place the loaf on a baking sheet cut side up and broil for 5 minutes or less, until golden. Serve immediately.

Serves 6 to 8.

Lasagna

*I*f you're a vegetarian, this recipe is also delicious without the meat. For a large crowd, try one of each.

BÉCHAMEL SAUCE
    4 tablespoons (½ stick) unsalted butter
    6 tablespoons flour
    2 cups milk
    Salt and pepper

Melt the butter in a heavy saucepan. Sprinkle in the flour and cook gently, stirring constantly with a whisk, for 5 minutes. Do not let the mixture brown or burn. In another saucepan warm the milk, then add it to the flour mixture, still stirring, until the mixture thickens. Add salt and pepper to taste and remove from the heat.

FILLING
    2 tablespoons olive oil
    1 pound ground meat (chicken, veal, or sweet or spicy sausages)
    1 large onion, diced
    Salt and pepper
    1 carrot, peeled and diced
    1 red bell pepper, seeded and diced
    1 yellow bell pepper, seeded and diced
    ½ cup corn kernels, fresh (from 1 ear) or canned and drained
    1 16-ounce can plum tomatoes with juice
    1 tablespoon chopped fresh thyme (or 1 teaspoon dried)
    1 tablespoon chopped fresh oregano (or 1 teaspoon dried)

Heat the olive oil in a large skillet (if you are using sausage, skip the oil). Add the meat, onion, and a little salt and pepper. Cover and cook over medium heat for 10 minutes. Add the carrot, bell peppers, and corn and cook, covered, for 5 minutes. Add the plum tomatoes and juice and bring the mixture to a boil. Stir in the herbs, then reduce the heat to simmer, cover, and cook for 30 minutes.

ASSEMBLY

    2 tablespoon olive oil
    1 box lasagna noodles
    ⅓ cup grated Parmesan cheese
    1 cup ricotta
    ½ pound mozzarella cheese, cut into ¼-inch slices

Preheat oven to 350 degrees.

Bring a large pot of water to a boil. Add the olive oil and lasagna noodles and cook according to the package directions. Drain and separate the strips, laying them out on waxed paper (they'll stick to paper towels).

Stir the Parmesan cheese and ricotta into the béchamel sauce.

Spread ½ cup of the meat filling over the bottom of a 9-x-13-inch casserole dish. Arrange 3 or 4 lasagna strips over the filling in a single layer. Top with a layer of the béchamel-cheese mixture, then a ladleful of the meat filling. Continue the layering process until you have 3 or 4 layers of lasagna strips. End with noodles and a coating of meat filling. Top with the sliced mozzarella.

Bake for 30 to 40 minutes. Let stand for 5 to 10 minutes before serving.

Serves 8 to 10.

Special-Occasion German Chocolate Cake

CAKE

    4 ounces sweetened chocolate, chopped

    1 cup (2 sticks) unsalted butter, softened

    2 cups sugar

    4 eggs, separated

    1 teaspoon vanilla extract

    2½ cups cake flour (not self-rising!)

    1 teaspoon baking soda

    ½ teaspoon salt

    1 cup buttermilk

    ½ teaspoon cream of tartar

Preheat oven to 350 degrees.

Butter and flour 3 9-inch round cake pans.

In a small bowl, combine the chocolate and ½ cup boiling water and stir occasionally until the chocolate melts and is smooth. In another bowl, cream the butter and slowly add the sugar, beating until fluffy. Beat in the egg yolks and vanilla, then the melted chocolate.

Sift the flour, baking soda, and salt together into a large bowl. Add them to the chocolate mixture, alternating with the buttermilk. In a separate bowl, beat the egg whites with a pinch of salt and the cream of tartar until they are just stiff. Spoon a large dollop of the whites into the batter and stir, then fold in the remaining whites.

Pour the batter into the 3 pans and bake for 30 to 40 minutes, until a toothpick inserted into the center comes away clean. Cool the layers for 20 minutes in the pans, then turn them out onto racks to cool completely.

FROSTING

    1 cup evaporated milk

    1 cup sugar

    3 egg yolks

8 tablespoons (1 stick) unsalted butter, cut into pieces
1 teaspoon vanilla extract
1 tablespoon brewed coffee
1⅓ cups shredded unsweetened coconut
1 cup chopped pecans

Place the evaporated milk, sugar, egg yolks, butter, vanilla, and coffee in a saucepan and cook over low heat, stirring constantly, until the mixture thickens, about 10 to 12 minutes. Do not boil! Remove from the heat and cool, stirring occasionally, then add the coconut and pecans.

When the layers are cool, spread the frosting on top of each and stack them, leaving the sides uncoated. The cake is best if served the next day at room temperature.

Serves 12.

BALLERINA'S BABY SHOWER

Baked Ham with Honey Mustard Glaze
Macaroni and Cheese
Tomato and Parmesan Salad
Meringue Bowl

Baby showers used to be an all-girl tradition, but I think I hosted my first shower at age nineteen! Now it's become a tradition: whenever a colleague or friend is expecting, we throw a party.

Two years ago our baby boom peaked. Several ballerinas in the company and Heather's sister Jennifer all had babies within three months of each other. Heather and I became pros, devising menus that satisfy children and adults alike, and discovering plain dishes that won't upset the mother-to-be. Here's an example.

J.S.

Baked Ham with Honey Mustard Glaze

I love serving ham because the leftovers are so useful—sandwiches, soups, jambalaya. Ham is dangerously addictive, however—be forewarned!

1 16-pound precooked ham
1 cup store-bought honey mustard
½ cup pineapple juice
½ cup red wine

Preheat oven to 350 degrees.

Place the ham in a roasting pan. Score the fat covering the outside in a checkerboard pattern, with 1-inch squares, about ¼ inch deep. Smear the honey mustard all over the outside. Pour the pineapple juice and red wine into the pan.

Bake for 1½ hours, basting often. Remove the ham from the oven and let it rest. Slice and serve at room temperature.

Serves 30.

Macaroni and Cheese

1 box macaroni elbows
2 cups shredded Cheddar cheese
1 cup shredded Monterey Jack cheese
½ cup grated Parmesan cheese
1½ cups milk
Salt and pepper

Preheat oven to 350 degrees.

In a large pot of boiling water, cook the macaroni noodles according to the package instructions. Don't overcook. Drain.

Grease a medium-size casserole dish. Combine the cheeses and milk, and salt and pepper to taste in a large mixing bowl (I like to use my hands) and pour into the casserole. Bake for 40 minutes, until the top is golden. Serve hot.

Serves 8.

Tomato and Parmesan Salad

6 large, very ripe tomatoes
Juice of 1 lemon
Salt and pepper
6 ounces Parmesan cheese
2 tablespoons chopped fresh chives
¼ cup olive oil

Core and slice the tomatoes, arranging the slices attractively on a large serving platter. Sprinkle with lemon juice and salt and pepper to taste. Shave curls of Parmesan cheese over the tomatoes, using a sharp paring knife or a vegetable peeler. Sprinkle with the chives, then drizzle with the olive oil.

Serves 6 to 8.

Meringue Bowl

8 egg whites, room temperature
Pinch cream of tartar
2 cups sugar
2 pints ice cream or sorbet, or 4 cups sliced fresh fruit, for filling

Preheat oven to 300 degrees.

In a dry bowl, beat the egg whites with the cream of tartar until stiff peaks form. Gradually beat in the sugar until the mixture becomes very shiny.

Line a baking sheet with parchment paper. Transfer the batter to the paper and shape it into a shallow bowl 10 to 12 inches in diameter. Bake for 15 minutes, then reduce the heat to 200 degrees and bake until the meringue turns light brown, another 45 to 60 minutes.

Cool completely, then transfer the meringue to a serving platter. Fill it with scooped ice cream or sorbet, or fresh fruit.

Serves 10 to 12.

V.

Global Gourmet

One of the many great things about living in New York is the availability of food from every corner of the earth. Whatever your palate desires—Chinese, Italian, Indian, French, Japanese, Mexican, or just American diner fare—it's never more than a few blocks away, and often available twenty-four hours a day.

Perhaps the reason we both like ethnic cuisine so much is that neither of us grew up in a stereotypically American hot-dogs-and-apple-pie kind of family. One of Jock's earliest memories is of his Navajo grandmother baking bread. Her hands were a blur as she kneaded the dough, shaping it into little rolls which she'd arrange on a big round peel his grandfather had carved from the trunk of a tree. He'd go outside and fire up the clay oven. When it was really hot she'd put the buns in, and half an hour later the world's most delicious bread emerged.

My mother was a young war bride from the north of England, who met my father when he was stationed there as a World War II glider pilot. They moved to Long Beach, California, where fresh fruit and vegetables were

abundant. But it was the 1950s, and canned fruit and frozen buttered vegetable medleys were considered the best that money could buy. My mother jokes that we were spared this all-American fate thanks to neighboring war brides from Italy, Ireland, and Spain. She swapped her mother's Yorkshire pudding recipe for a great spaghetti sauce, her mince pies for a rich Irish stew, and her watercress and banana sandwiches for a spicy paella.

Jock and I never tire of the food we grew up on, but our appetites have also been shaped by our travels and our friends. Some of these new recipes have become old favorites.

H. W.

SOTO FAMILY SOUTHWESTERN SPREAD

❋

Pop's Mom's Asopao
Mama Jo's Red Rice
Twice-as-Nice Barbecue Meat
Fried Bread

❋

My mom and dad came to our first annual Connecticut Fourth of July barbecue and stayed over, along with several other guests. When I got out of bed the next morning, I found my mom already busy in the kitchen. She sheepishly asked if she could fix lunch, and I said, "Please do!" since I was exhausted and felt as if I had been cooking for days. By midafternoon she had prepared a delicious meal. The aromas wafted through the house and lured everyone into the kitchen, where we feasted on an array of Latin and Navajo dishes.

It was a special treat for me, since this was the first time my parents had visited us in Connecticut. In a way, having my mom cook some of my favorite childhood recipes for us helped transform our house into a home. It was a blessing of sorts, and by far the best housewarming present I received.

J.S.

Pop's Mom's Asopao

2 pounds chicken parts, with skin
3 tablespoons recaito*
1 medium onion, chopped
2 cubes chicken bouillon
2 tablespoons adobo*
2 bags sasón*
1 teaspoon salt
1 small jar red pimento, chopped, and juice
1 cup tomato sauce or ketchup
¾ cup long-grain white rice
Available at Latin markets.

In a large stockpot, bring 4 quarts of water to a boil. Add the chicken parts and recaito. Cover and continue to boil over medium heat for 15 minutes. Add the chopped onion, bouillon cubes, adobo, sasón, and salt. (You may remove the chicken skin at this point, if you like.) Boil, covered, for 10 minutes. Add the pimento and juice, and tomato sauce or ketchup. Cover and boil for 10 minutes. Add the rice, return to a boil, then reduce the heat and simmer until the rice is cooked, about 20 minutes.

Serves 8.

Mama Jo's Red Rice

*I*t's a Puerto Rican tradition to serve white rice and beans with every meal, so when my parents were first married and living in Philadelphia, my dad's mother taught my mom how to make this important dish. To remind us of our Puerto Rican heritage, my dad insisted we have rice every night for dinner when I was growing up in Arizona. I hated it back then, because it was forced on me. Now I've grown to appreciate it and make it myself whenever I want to revisit the flavors of home.

3 tablespoons vegetable oil
1 medium onion, chopped
2 garlic cloves, minced
2 tablespoons recaito*
1½ tablespoons sasón*
1½ tablespoons adobo*
½ teaspoon salt
2 cups long-grain white rice
Optional: Vienna sausage, chopped kielbasa, canned red or black beans

Available at Latin markets.

In a large saucepan, heat the vegetable oil and sauté the onion and garlic until translucent. Add the recaito, sasón, adobo, and salt, and cook for 1 minute. At this point optionals may be added. (For beans, be sure to drain, rinse, and drain again before adding.)

Add the rice, stirring to mix well. Pour in enough hot water to cover the ingredients by at least ¾ inch. Bring the contents to a boil, stir once, and continue cooking until all of the water is absorbed. Cover the pot and turn the heat to low, steaming the contents for about 20 to 25 minutes, stirring once or twice.

Serves 6 to 8.

Twice-as-Nice Barbecue Meat

½ green bell pepper, cut into strips

½ red bell pepper, cut into strips

½ yellow bell pepper, cut into strips

1 large onion, sliced thin

Juice of 1 large lemon (2 to 3 tablespoons)

1 tablespoon vinegar (flavored, or your choice of red wine or balsamic)

2 tablespoons olive oil

2 tablespoons recaito*

1 to 2 tablespoons sasón*

1 tablespoon adobo*

1 teaspoon salt

6 to 7 large garlic cloves, minced

3 to 4 pounds cooked leftover red meat from barbecue (I usually use 1 to 2 pounds steak cut into strips, 1 pound crumbled hamburger, ½ to 1 pound crumbled sausage.)

Available at Latin markets.

In a medium bowl, combine the peppers, onion, lemon juice, vinegar, olive oil, recaito, sasón, adobo, salt, garlic, and ½ cup water. Pour the marinade into a flat dish, add the meat, and turn periodically to coat. Marinate for 2 hours at room temperature or overnight in the refrigerator.

Pour the marinade and meat into a large frying pan. Heat until the meat sizzles, then cover. Simmer for about 1 hour, until the meat is tender.

Serves 8.

Fried Bread

I grew up eating this Native American treat at home as well as at pow-wows, either sprinkled with powdered sugar or drizzled with honey. It's not dietetic, but it sure is good!

4 cups flour
3 teaspoons baking powder
½ cup powdered milk
1 teaspoon salt
1 tablespoon vegetable oil plus oil for frying

Combine all of the dry ingredients in a large bowl. Add 1 cup of warm water all at once and mix well. Add more warm water until a soft dough forms. Turn the dough out onto a clean, dry surface and begin kneading, adding additional flour if the dough becomes sticky. When the dough is smooth and elastic, add 1 tablespoon of oil and work it in a little, leaving the dough slightly moist. Place the dough in an oiled bowl in a warm spot, covered with a clean dishcloth, and let it rise for 1 to 2 hours.

Heat the vegetable oil in a heavy skillet until almost smoking. Pull off small balls (about 1½ inches in diameter) from the dough and roll them out to ¼ inch. Deep-fry the dough patties in vegetable oil, turning once, until golden. Drain on paper towels and serve immediately, with powdered sugar or honey, as desired.

Makes approximately 16 pastries, serving 8.

DANISH DINNER

✻

Glogg
Gule Aerter (Yellow Split-Pea Soup)
Frikadeller Meatballs
Sautéed Red Cabbage
Boiled Potatoes with Dill and Butter
Spiced Pear-Apple Sauce

✻

During the late 1970s, the New York City Ballet was performing at Tivoli Gardens in Copenhagen, Peter Martins's hometown. Mr. Balanchine had a long-standing affection for all things Danish—the choreography of Bournonville, the fountain and flowers of Tivoli Gardens, aquavit—but most of all he loved a hearty homemade Danish soup called *gule aerter*. He had been a ballet master with the Royal Danish Ballet in the thirties and reminisced so frequently about the wonderful meals he had in Copenhagen that, in celebration of his visit, Peter's mother prepared a magnificent Danish smorgasbord. From her tiny kitchen came course after course of true Danish delights. Although Tove Martins was nervous about having the great choreographer in her home, the meal was a triumph and Mr. Balanchine added it to his repertoire of wonderful Danish stories.

From time to time Jock and I prepare this whole feast. But feel free to use any or all of these recipes as you see fit. Skoal!

H. W.

Glogg

*T*his is a traditional Scandinavian drink, ideal for the holidays.

    1 bottle dry red wine
    1 cup Madeira
    1 tablespoon ground cardamom
    1 cinnamon stick
    Zest from ½ lemon, cut into strips
    ¼ cup firmly packed light brown sugar
    ¼ cup whole blanched almonds
    ½ cup raisins

In a large saucepan, combine the red wine and Madeira. Add the spices and bring to a simmer over low heat. Add the lemon zest and sugar, and stir to dissolve the sugar. Distribute the almonds and raisins among 4 cups and fill them with the wine.

Makes 4 cups, serving 6 to 8.

Gule Aerter (Yellow Split-Pea Soup)

1 pound small yellow split peas
2 pounds salt pork, cut into cubes
3 carrots, peeled and diced
1 large onion, chopped
2 leeks (white and light green part only), washed thoroughly and cut
    into quarters lengthwise
Salt and pepper
Dried thyme

In a large pot, soak the peas overnight in 1½ quarts of water.

Simmer the salt pork, covered, in 1½ quarts of water for 1½ hours to make broth (may be done a day ahead).

Boil the peas in the water they soaked in for 20 minutes, covered. Remove the lid and add the carrots, onion, and leeks and 1 quart of pork broth. Simmer, covered, for 2 to 3 hours. Add salt, pepper, and thyme to taste.

Serves 8.

Frikadeller Meatballs

1½ pounds lean ground pork or veal, or ¾ pound each, combined
1 egg
3 tablespoons flour
½ medium onion, grated
1 teaspoon salt
1 teaspoon pepper
¼ teaspoon ground nutmeg
1 cup milk
½ cup club soda
3 tablespoons unsalted butter

Combine all of the ingredients except the butter in a bowl (I usually use my hands). Form into meatballs using about 2 tablespoons of meat mixture for each.

Melt the butter in a large skillet and sauté the meatballs for about 5 to 10 minutes, until brown.

Serves 6.

Sautéed Red Cabbage

10 strips bacon, diced
1½ medium onions, cored and diced or sliced thin
1 medium head red cabbage, cored and diced or sliced thin
½ cup red wine
¼ cup red wine vinegar
1 tablespoon chopped fresh thyme (or 1 teaspoon dried)
½ cup golden raisins
Salt and pepper

In a large frying pan, cook the bacon until it's almost crisp. Pour off all but 4 tablespoons of fat. Add the onion and sauté until translucent, about 3 minutes. Stir in the cabbage, wine, vinegar, thyme, and raisins. Cover and cook over low heat until the cabbage wilts, adding salt and pepper to taste and stirring occasionally, about 40 minutes.

Serves 6.

Boiled Potatoes with Dill and Butter

18 small red potatoes
4 tablespoons (½ stick) unsalted butter
¼ cup chopped fresh dill
Salt and pepper

Scrub the potatoes and place them in a medium saucepan. Cover with water and bring to a boil. Simmer for 10 minutes, until the potatoes are soft (test with a fork). Drain.

In a large skillet, melt the butter. Add the potatoes, dill, and salt and pepper to taste. Sauté until well combined, about 3 minutes, and serve immediately.

Serves 6.

Spiced Pear-Apple Sauce

½ cup dry red wine
⅓ cup sugar
¼ cup fresh lemon juice
1 cinnamon stick
¼ teaspoon whole cloves
¼ teaspoon whole allspice
2 firm ripe Bosc pears, peeled, cored, and diced
2 large Granny Smith apples, peeled, cored, and diced
2 shallots, minced

Bring the wine, ½ cup water, sugar, and lemon juice to a boil in a large saucepan. Simmer, stirring, until the sugar dissolves. Tie the spices in a cheesecloth bag and add it to the pot. Simmer uncovered for 5 minutes.

Add the pears and apples to the syrup and simmer for 5 more minutes, stirring occasionally to make sure all the fruit is poached. Remove and discard the spice bag. Remove the pan from the heat and stir in the shallots.

Serve chilled or at room temperature.

Serves 6 to 8.

HEATHER'S CONDIMENT COLLECTION

*I*n southern California, we put everything from mayonnaise to Thousand Island dressing on a burger in addition to the basic lettuce, tomato, cheese, and onion. When I moved to New York City at the age of fifteen, I was shocked to discover that a hamburger or hot dog was often just that—either a small patty of beef or a boiled hot dog on a plain roll. Putting more than ketchup on either one was considered gourmet indeed.

Since Jock, Damian, and I bought the house together, I've been known as the "condiment queen." Sometimes our refrigerator is so stuffed with half-full jars that there's barely enough room for fresh food! My peculiar passion is responsible for such delicacies as *aspretto di pesca*, an aged peach vinegar I picked up in Rome, rose petal jam (Paris), pink grapefruit marmalade, spiced anchovy relish, and spicy dried-fig-and-date pickle! I may have a problem, but better safe than sorry.

You can start your own condiment collection with any (or all) of the following staples:

Grey Poupon Dijon mustard

Whole-grain mustard

Honey mustard

Hellmann's mayonnaise

Major Grey's chutney

Ketchup

Worcestershire sauce

Tabasco sauce

Peter Luger steak sauce

Assorted vinegars

Assorted oils

Fine-quality jams

Soy sauce

Vidalia onion relish

Newman's Own salsa

Dill pickles

Spanish capers

Assorted olives

Tapenade (olive spread)

Pickled beets

Newman's Own salad dressing

LOUISA, MARY, AND PETER'S TEX-MEX FIESTA

❉

Guacamole
Black Bean and Mango Salsa
Gazpacho
Pork and Beef Enchiladas
Chiles Rellenos

❉

Jock and I have danced all over America, and quite often in Jock's birthplace, New Mexico, but our performance schedule rarely allowed us to enjoy all the pleasures that make the Southwest so special. Several years ago, though, my dear friend Louisa Sarofim invited us to her gorgeous ranch and Jock and I were given the "tennis house," which is actually a wonderful little cottage overlooking a wildflower meadow. Two of my oldest and best friends, Mary Porter and Peter Wolff, and his daughter Natasha were also staying at Louisa's for the week. We all had a wonderful time hiking, lounging by Louisa's pool, going to the famed 10,000 Waves Spa, talking and laughing. Since Louisa lives part-time in Santa Fe, she knows the area well and took us nightly to her favorite local restaurants—El Nido, Santa Café, Escalera, and even the Tesuque Village Market. Each and every dinner was incredible, and to thank her for the fantastic trip, we decided on our last night to cook for her in the tennis house kitchen. Inspired by the unique Santa Fe atmosphere and cuisine, we thought, Why stop now?—and came up with an easy-to-fix, flavorful, and informal southwestern menu. With plenty of beer and a piñata on hand, we shared our last evening there with the dearest of friends having a great time over our very own Tex-Mex fiesta. Every time we make this meal we are transported back to Santa Fe, and say once again: *Muchas gracias,* Louisa! (For everything!)

H. W.

Guacamole

6 ripe avocados
Juice of 1 lemon
2 plum tomatoes, seeded and diced
1 small onion, diced
2 chili peppers, green or red
1 bunch cilantro
Tabasco sauce
Salt and pepper
1 tablespoon Hellmann's mayonnaise

Cut the avocados in half, remove the pits, and scrape the flesh into a bowl. Immediately stir in the lemon juice (this prevents the avocado from turning black). Add the tomatoes and onion. Carefully halve the chili peppers, discard the seeds, mince fine (I wear rubber gloves when doing this—and be sure to wash your hands before you touch your eyes!), and add them to bowl. Chop the cilantro and add it to the bowl.

Using a fork or potato masher, mix all of the ingredients until smooth. Add Tabasco to taste, one drop at a time—it's powerful stuff! Add salt and pepper, then stir in the mayonnaise. Serve immediately.

Serves 6 to 8.

Black Bean and Mango Salsa

1 16-ounce can black beans, drained
1 medium red onion, diced
1 large mango, peeled and diced
1 teaspoon paprika
½ tablespoon lemon juice
1 teaspoon balsamic vinegar
Tabasco sauce
Salt and pepper

In a medium bowl, combine the beans, onion, mango, paprika, lemon juice, and vinegar. Add Tabasco to taste, one drop at a time, as well as salt and pepper.

Serves 6 to 8.

Gazpacho

    8 ripe tomatoes
    2 medium red onions
    1 medium white onion
    2 large garlic cloves
    3 medium cucumbers
    1 red bell pepper
    1 yellow or orange bell pepper
    ½ cup red wine vinegar
    1 12-ounce can V8 juice
    Salt, pepper, and cayenne pepper
    Fresh dill sprigs for garnish

Peel, core, and coarsely chop all of the vegetables. Place them in a blender or food processor with the vinegar and V8—you may have to do this in 2 or 3 batches—and puree until almost smooth. Leave some chunks so the texture is a little bit crunchy. Refrigerate for at least 2 hours.

Add the seasonings to taste and serve the soup garnished with fresh dill sprigs.

Serves 8.

Pork and Beef Enchiladas

1 pound ground pork
1 pound ground beef
3 tablespoons olive or vegetable oil
1 large onion, finely chopped
2 garlic cloves, minced
½ teaspoon chili powder
1½ teaspoons cumin
2 teaspoons dried oregano
1 teaspoon red pepper flakes
1 8-ounce can corn, drained
1 15-ounce can crushed tomatoes
¼ cup chopped fresh cilantro
1 4-ounce can peeled and chopped green chili peppers
Juice of 1 lime
1 10-ounce can El Paso enchilada sauce
6 ounces (½ jar) Newman's Own salsa
Salt and pepper to taste
2 cups shredded Monterey Jack cheese
2 cups shredded sharp Cheddar cheese
8 10-ounce flour tortillas

In a large skillet, sauté the ground pork and beef in the oil until the meat begins to brown, about 5 minutes. Stir in the onion, garlic, chili powder, cumin, oregano, and red pepper flakes, and cook for another 5 minutes. Add the corn, crushed tomatoes, cilantro, green chili peppers, lime juice, enchilada sauce, salsa, and salt and pepper, and cook for 20 minutes.

In a bowl, combine the shredded cheeses.

Preheat oven to 350 degrees.

Spread ½ cup of the meat mixture over the bottom of a 9-x-13-inch casserole dish. With the dish lengthwise in front of you, lay one tortilla so that half of it is in the dish and the other half hangs over the left side. Spoon a thin line of the meat mixture and sprinkle a handful of cheese down the middle of the tortilla. Fold the right edge toward the middle to secure the filling, then roll the tortilla up from the right side, so the left side slips underneath. The enchilada should be nice and tight, with the seam on the bottom.

Lay the second tortilla so that its center is immediately to the right of the finished one. Fill it with the meat mixture and cheese and roll it up the same way. Continue until all of the tortillas are rolled up in the casserole dish.

Sprinkle half of the remaining cheese over the tortillas. Pour the remaining meat mixture over the cheese, then top with the rest of the cheese.

Bake for 20 to 30 minutes, until the top of the casserole is golden brown.

Serves 8.

Chiles Rellenos

10 fresh green chile relleno peppers (long, dark green), or 1 27-ounce
    can roasted, peeled whole green chiles
3 eggs
¾ cup flour
Vegetable oil for frying
½ pound grated Monterey Jack cheese

Broil the chile peppers, turning them occasionally, until their skin blackens (this may also be done over a gas flame, holding the peppers on a long fork). Place them in a paper bag or under an overturned bowl. When the peppers are cool, peel them, slit them down one side, and remove the seeds.

To make the batter, separate the eggs and beat the whites until they're stiff. Beat the yolks slightly and fold them into the whites. Fold in 3 tablespoons of flour.

Heat the vegetable oil in a heavy skillet until almost smoking.

For each chile, fill the cavity with grated cheese, roll it in the remaining flour, dip it in the batter, and fry until golden brown, turning once. Drain and serve.

Serves 10.

ITALIAN CHOLESTEROL BINGE

❄

Bruschetta
Fettuccine Carbonara
Tiramisù

❄

Many people are under the mistaken impression that dancers don't eat anything fattening. This meal should correct that misconception. While some of us (me) have to watch our weight more than others (Damian), the fact of the matter is that when you're dancing eight or ten hours a day, you burn off pretty much everything you eat.

Heather remembers one season when she was dancing so much that Mr. Balanchine became concerned she was getting too thin to go onstage. After rehearsal one day he called her into his office, sat her down, and presented her with a Tupperware container full of sliced bananas with fresh whipped cream and homemade cherry preserves. "A little something to fatten you up, my dear," he said, handing her a spoon. Heather didn't have the heart to tell him she hated bananas (especially with warm whipped cream!), and flattered by his concern, she pretended to enjoy this fattening concoction.

In my case, no one has ever suggested I put on a little weight. Though I was the last dancer hired by Mr. Balanchine and he cast me in several leading roles, he was no longer well enough to teach or rehearse me himself. Dancing his ballets and working in his company have given me great respect for him. But the stories that have made me love him are the ones Heather tells me while we share his passion for cooking.

If Mr. Balanchine were here today, I'm sure he'd advise me not to eat this meal too often. On the other hand, as he often said when we left rehearsal, *bon appétit!*

J.S.

Bruschetta

*T*his is best with summer tomatoes, although I have made it with plum tomatoes in the winter.

3 tablespoons olive oil
4 fresh tomatoes, seeded and diced
1 medium onion, diced
3 garlic cloves, minced
4 tablespoons chopped fresh oregano or basil
Salt and pepper
1 loaf Italian bread

Combine the olive oil, tomatoes, onion, garlic, and fresh herbs in a bowl. Season to taste with salt and pepper. Let the mixture stand at room temperature for about ½ hour, to allow flavors to combine.

Cut the bread into ½-inch slices and toast them under the broiler. Top the slices generously with the tomato mixture and serve as an appetizer.

Serves 8.

Fettuccine Carbonara

3 to 4 tablespoons olive oil

½ pound pancetta, cut into strips

1 medium onion, diced

16 ounces fettuccine

4 egg yolks

½ cup grated Parmesan cheese

2 tablespoons unsalted butter

Salt and pepper

Heat 2 tablespoons of the olive oil in a medium skillet and cook the pancetta until slightly brown. Add the onion and continue cooking until translucent. Remove the skillet from the heat.

Bring a large pot of salted water to a boil. Add the fettuccine and cook according to the package directions. Meanwhile, combine the egg yolks and grated cheese in a large serving bowl. When the pasta is cooked, drain and transfer it to the egg-cheese mixture. Toss the pasta with the butter, and salt and pepper to taste. If it gets gummy, add 1 to 2 tablespoons of olive oil. Stir in the pancetta and onion, and serve.

Serves 4.

Tiramisù

One Thanksgiving, Jane Wilson asked me to bring a dessert. I decided to knock everybody's socks off with tiramisù, figuring it would be elegant enough to impress even this crowd of sophisticated gourmands. After consulting several recipes, I went to the nearest gourmet store and scanned the refrigerated case for mascarpone cheese. All out. Cheese is cheese, I thought. I'll just substitute. "I'll take that one," I said to the man behind the counter, pointing to a slab of Gorgonzola. Back home, when I made the tiramisù it didn't achieve the exact consistency I was aiming for. So I wrapped it in foil and stuck it in the freezer for a couple of hours.

On the way uptown to Jane's house, I began to suspect something had gone wrong. An ominous sloshing sound emerged from the serving dish, but I steadfastly ignored it. Dinner was fabulous, as always, but as dessert approached, I couldn't shake a sense of impending doom. When the dishes were cleared, Jane took the tiramisù out of the refrigerator and uncovered it. The smell was overwhelmingly repulsive. She gallantly tried to serve this mess, but nobody was foolish enough to partake. Jane quickly substituted vanilla ice cream topped with amaretto. Somebody suggested I follow a recipe next time; I now pass that advice on to you.

3 egg yolks
1½ tablespoons sugar
4 tablespoons dark rum
½ pound mascarpone
1½ cups strong espresso, cooled
24 ladyfingers
Semisweet chocolate shavings

Beat the egg yolks and sugar until light. Add 2 tablespoons of the rum and the mascarpone and beat until smooth. Add 2 tablespoons of the espresso and mix well.

Add the remaining rum and espresso to the bottom of a baking dish and arrange the ladyfingers in a single layer. Spoon the mascarpone mixture over the ladyfingers and cover the dish with plastic wrap. Refrigerate for at least 30 minutes. Before serving, sprinkle with chocolate shavings.

Serves 8.

LOIS, LINDY, AND LESLIE'S LOUISIANA DINNER

Crawfish Étouffée
Angel Wings
Corn Maque Choux

❋

Melinda and Leslie Roy are sisters who both had wonderful careers dancing with the New York City Ballet. They're from Lafayette, Louisiana, and although they've lived north of the Mason-Dixon line for more than half their lives, they still sound as if they just stepped out of the bayou. Several years ago they retired from the company and moved upstate. Lindy founded a country-western dance troupe called the Outlaws, and Leslie and their mother, Lois, opened a ballet school and shop in Saratoga Springs.

Last summer, when we were performing in Saratoga, they invited us to dinner and served a real Louisiana feast. If you're in the mood for a sultry southern soiree, put on some jazz, turn off the air-conditioning, and try the following recipes.

H. and J.

Crawfish Étouffée

Serve this dish over steamed white rice.

  3 tablespoons vegetable oil
  1 tablespoon butter
  3 tablespoons flour
  1 medium onion, diced fine
  ½ cup diced red bell pepper
  ½ cup diced celery
  3 garlic cloves, pressed
  2 pounds peeled crawfish
  Salt and cayenne pepper
  3 tablespoons chopped fresh parsley
  3 tablespoons chopped scallion tops (green parts)

In a heavy-bottomed pot, combine the oil, butter, and flour over low heat to make a roux. Continue stirring and cooking until the roux reaches a dark caramel color, about 25 minutes. Add the onion, bell pepper, celery, and garlic and cook until the vegetables soften, 10 to 15 minutes, stirring every few minutes. Add 1 cup of water, cover, and simmer for 1 hour.

Add the crawfish and cook uncovered for 20 to 30 minutes. Season liberally with salt and cayenne pepper. Stir in the parsley and scallion tops and cook for 5 minutes more.

Serves 4 to 6.

Angel Wings

2 pounds chicken wings
½ cup plain yogurt
4 tablespoons lemon juice
1 tablespoon Dijon mustard
3 garlic cloves, pressed
1 teaspoon salt
½ teaspoon dried sage
½ teaspoon dried oregano
Black and cayenne pepper
½ cup bread crumbs
½ cup grated Parmesan cheese
2 tablespoons unsalted butter, melted

Rinse the chicken wings in cold water and pat them dry. Trim the tips.

In a ceramic or glass bowl combine the yogurt, lemon juice, mustard, garlic, salt, sage, oregano, and black and cayenne pepper to taste (the marinade should be a bit spicy). Add the wings and toss to coat. Cover and refrigerate for at least 3 hours, preferably overnight.

In a paper or plastic bag, combine the bread crumbs, Parmesan cheese, and more salt, cayenne pepper, and black pepper to taste. Transfer a few wings at a time to the bag and shake to coat. Arrange the coated wings on a well-greased cookie sheet. When all of the wings are coated, cover with plastic wrap and refrigerate at least 3 hours.

Preheat oven to 375 degrees.

Remove the wings from the fridge. Drizzle with the melted butter and bake for 30 minutes, until golden brown.

Serves 4 to 6.

Corn Maque Choux

8 ears fresh corn, shucked
2 tablespoons vegetable oil
2 tablespoons unsalted butter
¾ cup diced onion (1 medium onion)
¼ cup diced red bell pepper
¾ cup chopped ripe tomatoes
Salt and cayenne pepper

With a serrated knife, cut the kernels from the corncobs and scrape the cobs to collect the pulp and milk of the corn.

Heat the oil and butter in a large skillet. Add the corn, pulp, and juice, along with the onion, bell pepper, and tomatoes, and stir to mix. Reduce the heat to low, cover, and cook for 1 hour, stirring every few minutes so the vegetables don't stick to the bottom. Season generously with salt and cayenne pepper.

Serves 4 to 6.

VI.

Country Cooking

As much as we love New York, some of our fondest memories are of weekends spent relaxing at friends' homes outside the city. When, in 1993, we decided, along with Damian, to buy our own country home, we gravitated toward the northwest corner of Connecticut, an exquisite, rural landscape where we'd spent many happy times over the years.

We quickly found just the right house only two hours from the city, on twenty acres with a big open kitchen and lots of room for guests. It was a new house, and parts of it were unfinished when we bought it. While we all three share in the gardening, most of the time when we're indoors cooking, Damian can be found repairing a fence or building something in his workshop.

The main ingredient in all our cooking is simplicity: our primary goal is relaxation, spending time outdoors enjoying the company of our friends. The menus that follow reflect this notion by keeping preparation and cooking time to a minimum. We've found the barbecue to be a godsend—it

makes everything taste great and there's virtually no cleanup afterward. The fresher the ingredients are, the better—locally grown produce and good cuts of meat, poultry, or fish need very little fussing to bring out their naturally delicious flavors.

Even in the city, you can put a barbecue on the terrace (or an illicit hibachi on the fire escape) and try these menus anytime you're in the mood for a casually elegant evening. Just invite a few friends over, toss together a couple of these dishes, mix a pitcher of sangria, and have fun!

H. and J.

FOURTH OF JULY BARBECUE

❉

Grilled Shrimp
Barbecued Chicken
Marinated Steak
Grilled Corn on the Cob
All-American Potato Salad
Greek Salad
Grilled Fruit

❉

The first summer after we bought our house we had a huge house-warming party over the Fourth of July weekend. I cooked this huge surf 'n' turf meal—enough food for an army—but when more and more people kept showing up, I began to worry that we might actually run out!

Since then, we've made the Fourth of July barbecue a tradition. Friends arrive at about three in the afternoon and stay as long as they like, even overnight. While the crowd changes slightly from one year to the next, the menu doesn't. I've thought about modifying it, but our guests say they like it just as it is—which is fine by me. That way I have more time to spend enjoying the holiday.

J.S.

Grilled Shrimp

We've found that when you serve a variety of entrees, people would rather have a little of everything. So we cut the steaks or fish in half or thirds and plan on a couple of shrimp per person.

24 jumbo shrimp, heads and tails cut off
¼ cup minced red bell pepper
¼ cup minced yellow bell pepper
3 garlic cloves, minced
Juice of 4 limes
2 shallots, minced
3 dashes Tabasco sauce
2 tablespoons olive oil
Salt and pepper
½ cup tequila
1 tablespoon chopped fresh parsley
1 tablespoon chopped fresh cilantro

Prepare the barbecue.

Rinse the shrimp and drain them on paper towels. Combine all of the ingredients in a large bowl and marinate the shrimp at room temperature for 1 hour.

Remove the shrimp from the marinade and thread them on skewers. Cook them on a hot grill for 3 minutes on each side.

Serves 12 as an hors d'oeuvre, or 3 to 4 as a main course.

Barbecued Chicken

18 chicken legs with thighs attached
Salt and pepper
2 12-ounce cans beer
1 tablespoon chopped fresh oregano (or 1 teaspoon dried)
1 tablespoon chopped fresh thyme (or 1 teaspoon dried)
2 cups red wine vinegar
⅔ cup ketchup
⅓ cup brown sugar
¼ cup honey
1 tablespoon cumin
1 tablespoon soy sauce
1 teaspoon tomato paste
4 tablespoons olive oil
1 teaspoon paprika
1 teaspoon cayenne pepper
1 medium onion, minced

Preheat oven to 350 degrees.

Rinse the chicken legs in cold water and pat them dry with paper towels. Place the legs in a large roasting pan and season them to taste with salt and pepper. Add the beer and sprinkle with the oregano and thyme. Bake for 45 minutes.

While the chicken cooks and cools, combine the remaining ingredients in a large pan. When the chicken is room temperature, add it to the marinade and toss to coat. Cover with plastic wrap and chill for 2 hours.

Prepare the barbecue. Remove the chicken from the refrigerator and grill it for 10 minutes on each side.

Serves 18.

Marinated Steak

2 tablespoons Dijon mustard
½ cup olive oil
2 tablespoons soy sauce
½ cup ketchup
5 garlic cloves, minced
1 medium onion, minced
1 tablespoon Worcestershire sauce
½ cup red wine vinegar
Ground black pepper
6 8-ounce shell steaks, about 1 inch thick

Stir together all of the ingredients except the steak in a large bowl.

Rinse the steaks under cold water and pat them dry. Arrange the steaks in a shallow dish or roasting pan and cover them with the marinade, turning to coat. Marinate for 2 hours at room temperature or overnight in the refrigerator.

Fire up the grill. Grill the steaks for 7 minutes on the first side and 5 minutes on the second side, for rare.

Serves 6, generously.

Grilled Corn on the Cob

16 ears fresh corn
8 tablespoons (1 stick) unsalted butter, softened
Salt and pepper

There are two ways to grill corn on the cob, in the husk, or in aluminum foil. In the husk makes for a more dramatic presentation, but it's slightly more trouble than in foil. Both methods are scrumptious.

To grill in the husk, peel back the husks without removing them entirely, and pull off all of the silk threads. Smear each ear with ½ tablespoon butter, salt and pepper generously, then pull the husks back up to cover the ears. Grill for 10 minutes, turning frequently.

To grill in foil, remove the husks and threads altogether, butter and season the corn as described above, and wrap each ear in the foil. Grill for 10 minutes, turning frequently.

Serves 8.

All-American Potato Salad

6 pounds red potatoes, scrubbed and quartered

¼ teaspoon freshly ground black pepper

1 cup thinly sliced red onion

1 cup sliced celery

½ red bell pepper, diced

½ yellow bell pepper, diced

½ orange bell pepper, diced

2 cups Hellmann's mayonnaise

5 tablespoons Dijon mustard

3 tablespoons chopped fresh tarragon

8 hard-boiled eggs, peeled and quartered

Bring a pot of salted water to a boil. Add the potatoes and cook until tender yet still firm, about 10 minutes. Drain.

Combine all of the ingredients in a large bowl and toss to mix. Refrigerate and serve cold.

Serves 16.

Greek Salad

Back when Ulrik and I were still in our floor-through apartment on Eighteenth Street, we used to spend the month of August in Greece. A whole gang of us would get together and rent a house—me, Ulrik, John, Jane, and Julia, Bruce Padgett, and a couple of Ulrik's Danish friends. The second year, Heather showed up for a week, as well; she was traveling in Europe and just decided to drop by.

We usually ate out, because the food was so inexpensive and good, but when we ate at home, Jane did most of the cooking. I remember once she marinated calamari in olive oil, lemon juice, vinegar, and all these onions and peppers. She put it in the refrigerator overnight and the next day it was unbelievably delicious.

Whenever I want to remind myself of those sunny summer days in Greece, I throw together this salad and it takes me right back.

8 ripe medium tomatoes, cut into bite-sized pieces
4 to 6 large cucumbers, peeled, seeded, and cut into bite-sized pieces
1½ cups diced Feta cheese
1 medium red onion, diced
1 green bell pepper, diced
20 Greek olives
3 tablespoons olive oil
Juice of 1 lemon
1 tablespoon chopped fresh oregano (or 1 teaspoon dried)
Salt and pepper

Place the tomatoes, cucumbers, cheese, onion, bell pepper, and olives in a salad bowl. Drizzle with the olive oil and lemon juice, sprinkle with the oregano, add salt and pepper to taste (more pepper than salt), then toss to combine.

Serves 10 to 12.

Grilled Fruit

*H*ere's a simple yet elegant way to end a barbecue dinner. You don't want the coals too hot, or they'll burn the fruit; they should be just hot enough to caramelize the natural sugars.

A selection of the following fruits:
Fresh pineapple, peeled and cut into ¾-inch rings
Mangoes, halved with pits removed
Peaches, halved with pits removed
Nectarines, halved with pits removed
Apricots, halved with pits removed
Bananas, peeled and sliced lengthwise
Vanilla ice cream (optional)
Pound cake (optional)

After the flames have died down, arrange the fruit on the grill, skin side up. Turn the fruit when the natural sugars begin to caramelize, anywhere from 5 to 10 minutes depending on the heat of the coals and the size of the fruit. When both sides are cooked, remove the fruit from the heat and serve plain or over pound cake, vanilla ice cream, or both.

JENN'S LOBSTER DINNER

❁

Boiled Lobster
Corn on the Cob with Chive-Garlic Butter
Cynthia's Salad

❁

The first summer we had our house in Connecticut, it was the only place we wanted to be. There was so much to be done to make it ours, and we threw ourselves into it with gusto. As often happens, life intrudes on such single-minded pursuits—one of our good friends invited us to her wedding in Southampton, so we dropped our hammers and shovels, and off we went to Long Island. It was a dramatic and elegant gathering overlooking the Atlantic Ocean, and we were all glad to be there to share in Rita and Ian's happiness.

As it happens, this interruption in our work schedule provided us with lots of good ideas. We found ourselves taking extra note of the gardens and architecture we saw and, of course, the food we tasted. We started our trip back full of ideas and fantasies for our home. As we drove, one of the familiar sights of an August in the Northeast appeared—signs for fresh lobster every few miles along the roadside. I immediately thought of my sister Jennifer, who adores lobster. I could almost hear the cracking of claws, and knew what a great return dinner we would share. It's a joy to make a meal for someone you love; here is the meal we made for my Jenn.

H. W.

Boiled Lobster

*T*here's nothing a few herbs and spices can't improve. This lobster recipe is a case in point.

2 tablespoons black peppercorns

6 lemons, halved

3 cups white wine or beer

4 bay leaves

12 garlic cloves, smashed

4 tablespoons chopped fresh tarragon (or 4 teaspoons dried)

4 tablespoons chopped fresh oregano (or 4 teaspoons dried)

4 tablespoons chopped fresh thyme (or 4 teaspoons dried)

4 medium onions, quartered

2 tablespoons paprika

2 tablespoons cayenne pepper

6 1½-pound lobsters

12 tablespoons (1½ sticks) unsalted butter

Fill two large stockpots (at least 6-quart) two thirds full of water. To each pot add 1 tablespoon of peppercorns, 6 lemon halves, 1½ cups of white wine or beer, 2 bay leaves, 2 tablespoons of salt, 6 smashed garlic cloves, 2 tablespoons each of fresh tarragon, oregano, and thyme (or 2 teaspoons dried), 2 quartered onions, and 1 tablespoon each paprika, cayenne pepper, and cumin. Bring to a rolling boil.

Drop 3 live lobsters into each pot, cover, and boil for 10 minutes. If you're squeamish about hearing the lobsters knocking around in the pot, you may want to leave the room. Remove, drain, and prepare to earn your supper! The cracking is hard work but worth it. Serve with melted butter as dipping sauce.

Serves 6.

Corn on the Cob with Chive-Garlic Butter

1 stick unsalted butter, softened
2 garlic cloves, minced
1 tablespoon minced fresh chives
2 tablespoons salt
12 ears fresh corn, husked

In a small bowl mash the garlic and chives into the softened butter. Transfer the mixture to an 8-ounce ramekin, smoothing the top with a knife or rubber spatula. Press a piece of waxed paper so that it sticks to the top, and place the herb butter in the refrigerator to harden and chill, at least one hour.

Bring a large stockpot of water to a rolling boil. Add the salt and corn. Boil for 5 to 10 minutes, depending on the freshness of the corn and the size of the kernels.

Drain and serve with the chive-garlic butter.

Serves 6.

Cynthia's Salad

I love this salad, but never as much as when Cynthia adds her own special touch.

CROUTONS

    ½ loaf French or Italian bread
    ¼ cup olive oil
    2 cloves garlic, minced

Preheat oven to 350 degrees.

Cut the bread into 12 ¼-inch slices. With a pastry brush or paper towel, coat one side of each slice with olive oil. Place the slices on a baking sheet. Sprinkle the oiled bread with garlic. Bake for 10 minutes, until bread toasts, making sure the garlic doesn't burn.

SALAD

    3 garlic cloves, crushed
    ½ cup olive oil
    1 tablespoon Dijon mustard
    2 tablespoons red wine vinegar
    2 heads Bibb lettuce, washed and spun dry
    4 hard-boiled eggs, sliced
    3 ripe tomatoes, sliced
    6 slices cooked bacon, crumbled

In a small bowl, blend the crushed garlic, olive oil, mustard, and vinegar. Place the lettuce in a large salad bowl. Top with the sliced eggs and tomatoes, and the crumbled bacon. Add the vinaigrette and toss to coat.

Serve with the croutons.

Serves 6 to 8.

ODE TO PAUL NEWMAN

Paul Newman is a genuine American icon. A wonderful actor with great personal charisma, he has illuminated our lives through his many roles. Who could forget his Brick in *Cat on a Hot Tin Roof*, his Butch Cassidy, or the aging hustler in *The Color of Money*?

For most people, this would be accomplishment enough, but Paul Newman is not only a superstar but a great American hero as well. For years he has also had a quiet second career running a successful business called Newman's Own. From the modest beginnings of a pasta sauce and a salad dressing, he has built a food empire which manufactures three different salsas, five pasta sauces, four salad dressings, three popcorns, and my personal favorite, Newman's Own lemonade. All of the proceeds go to charity.

The far-reaching effect of the $78 million he has donated can never be measured. He runs a camp for terminally ill children and an antidrug program, and funds countless arts, health, and educational programs across the country. His generosity is overwhelming and should be an inspiration to all of us. So when you reach for a salsa, a pasta sauce, a salad dressing, popcorn, or a carton of lemonade, buy Newman's Own and help him to help others.

SIX SIMPLE SUPPERS

❋

Chicken Curry
Saffron Rice

Broccoli and Asparagus Soup
Flounder Ipswich Style
Beet and Goat Cheese Salad
Applesauce Tart

Seared Tuna with Asparagus and Mesclun
Rice Salad
Peach Upside-Down Cake

Grilled Mahimahi
Avocado, Snow Pea, and Walnut Salad
Heather's Mom's Lemon Meringue Pie

Roast Leg of Lamb
Mint Chutney
Cynthia's Potatoes
Salad with Faux Benihana Vinaigrette
Judy Tomkin's Almond Cake

Red Pepper and Fennel Soup
Soft-Shell Crabs
Zucchini Gratin
Fruit Cobbler

❋

*I*n the summertime we eat outside as much as we can, either on the porch or on the lawn. Our house sits atop a hill, so on clear nights we enjoy breathtaking sunsets. In the winter, we often picnic indoors, serving the meal buffet-style in the kitchen, then eating around the fireplace in the living room.

Because we usually have the whole day free before a dinner party in the country, we have time to make desserts from scratch. Even so, you'll find none of the dessert recipes are terribly complicated. Much as we love to cook, when we're on vacation we don't want to spend hours cooped up in the kitchen when we could be reading, gardening, or doing nothing at all.

H. and J.

Chicken Curry

Chicken Curry with Saffron Rice is a quick meal that we learned from our good friend Anne Bass. She likes to serve this as the centerpiece of an informal buffet for large groups of people.

3 pounds chicken, preferably breasts and thighs, or better yet, boneless
Flour for dusting
4 tablespoons unsalted butter
3 medium onions, diced
1 garlic clove, minced
2 tablespoons curry powder
2 cups low-sodium or homemade chicken broth
2 tablespoons Major Grey's chutney, chopped
½ cup raisins
2 tart apples, peeled, cored, and sliced
½ teaspoon powdered ginger
½ teaspoon salt
¼ cup blanched almonds, chopped
½ cup heavy cream
Juice of ½ lemon

Rinse the chicken parts in cold water and pat them dry with paper towels. Remove the meat from the bones and dice. Heat 3 tablespoons of the butter in a skillet. Dust the chicken pieces in flour, then place them in the skillet and sauté until lightly browned on all sides. Transfer to a plate and keep warm.

To the butter remaining in the skillet add the onions and garlic and sauté until golden. Remove from heat.

In a large saucepan melt 2 teaspoons of the butter. Add the curry powder and stir until the mixture is smooth. Add the chicken broth, chutney, raisins, apples, ginger, and salt. Bring to a boil, then cover, reduce heat, and simmer for 30 minutes.

Meanwhile, sauté the almonds in the remaining teaspoon of butter until they are golden. Transfer to a mortar and grind with a pestle. Heat the cream in a small saucepan—don't let it boil! Stir in the almond paste and cook for 5 minutes.

Add the almond cream, sautéed onions and garlic, and chicken to the sauce. Simmer for 15 minutes, until thickened. Add the lemon juice and serve.

Serves 6.

Saffron Rice

2 tablespoons olive oil
1 medium red onion, chopped
3 garlic cloves, minced
1 red or orange bell pepper, diced
2 cups basmati rice, rinsed
1 tablespoon chopped fresh thyme (or 1 teaspoon dried)
Salt and pepper
4 cups low-sodium or homemade chicken broth, or water
Pinch of saffron threads

In a 1-quart saucepan, heat the olive oil and sauté the onion, garlic, and bell pepper until the onion is translucent, about 5 minutes. Add the rice and stir to coat with oil. Add the thyme, salt and pepper to taste, and broth or water. Bring to a boil, then turn down the heat, cover the pot, and simmer for about 18 minutes, until just a little liquid remains. Stir in the saffron and cook for another few minutes, until the liquid is completely absorbed. Remove from the heat and let the rice sit covered a few minutes before serving.

Serves 6.

Broccoli and Asparagus Soup

4 tablespoons (½ stick) unsalted butter
4 garlic cloves, chopped
1 medium red onion, diced
1 medium Idaho potato, peeled and diced
1 cup chopped asparagus
8 cups chopped broccoli florets
8 cups low-sodium or homemade chicken broth
Juice of 1 lemon
Salt and pepper

Melt the butter in a large stockpot. Add the garlic, onion, and potato, and sauté for 5 minutes. Add the asparagus and broccoli and the broth and bring to a boil. Reduce the heat, cover the pot, and simmer until the vegetables are tender, about 30 minutes. Puree the soup in batches in a blender or food processor, or with a hand-held blender. Return it to the pot, and add the lemon juice and salt and pepper to taste.

Serves 8.

Flounder Ipswich Style

*D*amian's godfather, Abdo, taught us this recipe. Off the coast near Ipswich, Massachusetts, fishermen catch flounder in Plum Island Sound. Abdo would often take Damian and his brother Jonathan fishing all morning, then stop on Plum Island for a swim on the way home. For dinner he'd cook up the day's catch, Ipswich style.

2½ pounds lean flounder filets (sole and perch work nicely too)
Salt and pepper
4½ tablespoons unsalted butter, softened
2 tablespoons minced shallots or scallions
⅔ cup white wine or vermouth
4 tablespoons flour
1 cup milk

Preheat oven to 350 degrees.

Rinse the fish fillets under cold water and pat them dry with paper towels. Lightly score the milky side of the fillets with a sharp knife, to keep them from curling. Season both sides with salt and pepper to taste.

Grease a 9-x-13-inch ovenproof dish with ½ tablespoon of the butter and sprinkle the shallots or scallions over the bottom. Arrange the fillets, slightly overlapping, in a single layer on top of the shallots or scallions. Pour in the wine or vermouth and enough water (or fish stock, if you have it) to almost cover the fish. Dot the tops of the fish with 1 tablespoon of the butter.

Place the baking dish on top of 2 burners and bring the contents to a boil. Carefully transfer the dish to the oven. Bake for 8 to 10 minutes, until the fish is milky white and slightly resistant to the touch, *not* dry and flaky.

Transfer the fish to a platter, cover with foil, and keep warm.

Boil down the fish-poaching liquid until it is reduced to about 1 cup. Meanwhile, in a medium saucepan melt the remaining 3 tablespoons of butter and blend in the flour, stirring with a whisk, until smooth. Remove from the heat, add the fish-poaching liquid, and whisk vigorously. Return the contents of the saucepan to a simmer and gradually add the milk until the sauce becomes thick enough to coat a spoon.

Distribute the fish among the plates and spoon the sauce around the edges.

Serves 6.

Beet and Goat Cheese Salad

8 to 10 medium beets (Try to get them all about the same size.)

1½ tablespoons red wine vinegar

3 tablespoons olive oil

¼ pound fresh goat cheese, crumbled (or more, if you like it as much
as we do!)

Freshly ground black pepper

Preheat oven to 350 degrees.

Scrub the beets, trim off the stems and roots, then bake the beets on a baking sheet in the oven for 45 minutes to 1 hour. Cool, peel, and julienne the beets.

In a serving bowl, toss the beets with the vinegar and olive oil. Cover and chill. Before serving, top with the goat cheese and freshly ground pepper to taste.

Serves 6 to 8.

Applesauce Tart

CRUST

    1 to 1¼ cups flour

    7 tablespoons unsalted butter, chilled and cut into pieces

    2 teaspoons sugar

    ⅛ teaspoon salt

    3 tablespoons ice water

Place 1 cup of flour, the butter, sugar, and salt in a bowl of a food processor fitted with a metal blade. Process just until the mixture resembles coarse crumbs, about 10 seconds. Add the water little by little, slowly pulsing after each addition, until the pastry begins to hold together (you may not need all 3 tablespoons of water, but you certainly won't need more).

The second the dough forms a ball, stop processing and turn the dough out onto waxed paper. Mold it into a biscuit shape. If the dough is excessively sticky, sprinkle with a tablespoon or two of flour. Wrap the dough in waxed paper and refrigerate it for at least one hour.

FILLING

    8 Granny Smith apples, peeled, cored, and chopped

    ½ cup apple cider

    4 tablespoons (½ stick) unsalted butter

Place the apples, cider, and butter in a large saucepan. Cover and cook over medium heat, stirring occasionally, until the apples soften, about 15 minutes. Puree in a blender or food processor.

ASSEMBLY

    2 Granny Smith apples, peeled, cored, and sliced into thin wedges

    ¼ cup apricot jam

    1 tablespoon cognac

Preheat oven to 350 degrees.

Remove the dough from the refrigerator and on a well-floured surface roll it out to ⅛-inch thickness. Transfer to a 10-inch fluted tart pan with a removable bottom. Press the dough into the corners of the pan and trim the edges (the easiest way to do this is to roll the pin across the top of the fluted edges, neatly cutting off the overhang). Place dried beans or pie weights in the center of the dough and bake for 10 minutes.

Take the shell out of the oven and remove the weights. Spoon in the applesauce filling until it is nearly flush with the top of the crust. Reserve the remaining applesauce for another use (it's delicious with pork or roasted chicken). Arrange the sliced apples decoratively to cover the entire tart. Place the tart in the oven and bake for 30 minutes, until the apples and crust turn golden.

Meanwhile, melt the jam in a small saucepan over low heat. Strain it, then return it to the pan and add the cognac. Stir to combine.

When the tart is cooked, remove it from the oven and cool it on a baking rack. With a pastry brush, paint the top with the apricot glaze. When the tart is completely cool, remove the sides from the pan. Dampen one sheet of a paper towel, fold it into a square, and place it in the center of a cake plate. Set the tart on top—this little trick will keep the bottom of the pan from slipping when you slice the tart.

Serves 8 to 10.

MIX-AND-MATCH SOUPS

*I*f there's one thing I feel confident making without a recipe and without Jock's help, it's soup. I like to make large batches and freeze it in quart-sized containers so that I always have some on hand. This is especially convenient in the country: when we arrive late at night we just pull a couple of containers out, defrost them in a pot on the stove, and in minutes have steaming bowls of home-made soup.

For years I'd been diligently following recipes and measuring ingredients, when it dawned on me one day that all pureed vegetable soups are essentially the same. All you need are vegetables, one or more flavoring agents, a thickener, broth, and enough imagination and culinary sense to predict which flavors will complement each other. If you've got an hour to spare, try mixing and matching some of the ingredients suggested below—or add your own.

VEGETABLES	FLAVORINGS	THICKENER	BROTH
Carrots	Garlic	Idaho potato	Low-sodium or homemade chicken
Broccoli	Onion	Heavy cream	
Parsnips	Shallot	Yogurt	Low-sodium or homemade beef
Squash	Scallion		
Mushrooms	Parsley		Homemade or canned vegetable
Cauliflower	Thyme		Canned tomatoes
Celery	Oregano		Water
Leeks	Tarragon		
Fennel	Dill		
Asparagus	Bay leaf		
	Ginger		
	Curry		

Basic Steps

Select and chop the vegetables and flavoring agents. If you choose potatoes as your thickener, peel and chop a couple of Idaho potatoes. Heat a few tablespoons of olive oil in a large stockpot. When hot but not smoking, add the vegetables and flavorings and sauté for 5 minutes. Add enough broth to cover the vegetables comfortably and turn the heat to high. When the soup comes to a boil, reduce the heat and simmer, covered, until the vegetables are cooked, about 45 minutes.

Remove the bay leaf if used for flavoring, and transfer the soup to a blender or food processor, or use my all-time favorite gadget, a hand-held blender, to puree. Return to the pot and season to taste with salt and pepper. (If you choose to use heavy cream as a thickener, add it right before serving—never freeze soup with heavy cream or yogurt bases.)

Seared Tuna with Asparagus and Mesclun

FISH

    8 6-ounce tuna steaks, about 1½ inches thick

    3 lemons

    ⅓ cup white wine

    ⅓ cup Worcestershire sauce

    2 tablespoons soy sauce

    Salt and pepper

    4 garlic cloves, minced

    2 teaspoons cumin

    ¼ cup chopped fresh tarragon (or 4 teaspoons dried)

Prepare the grill.

Rinse the tuna, pat it dry with paper towels, and place the steaks in a single layer in a shallow dish. Squeeze the lemons over the fish.

In a bowl combine all of the remaining ingredients. Pour over the fish and turn to coat. Marinate for 20 minutes.

Grill for 7 minutes on the first side, 5 on the second, for medium rare.

ASSEMBLY

    40 asparagus stalks, washed and trimmed

    8 cups mesclun lettuce

    24 cherry tomatoes, halved

    7 tablespoons olive oil

    4 tablespoons rice wine vinegar

    1½ teaspoons sugar

    1½ teaspoons soy sauce

    3 garlic cloves, minced

    2½ teaspoons minced ginger

    1 red onion, sliced

Steam the asparagus for 5 minutes, then transfer quickly to ice water to stop the asparagus from cooking any more and keep it from turning khaki-colored.

Place 1 cup of mesclun on each plate. Slice each tuna steak into strips and fan it atop the mesclun. Drape 5 asparagus stalks and scatter 6 cherry tomato halves over each tuna steak.

In a bowl stir the olive oil, vinegar, sugar, soy sauce, garlic, and ginger to blend. Add the onion slices and toss to coat. Ladle the onion vinaigrette over the tuna.

Serves 8.

Rice Salad

2 cups uncooked white rice
4 cups low-sodium or homemade chicken broth
½ cucumber, peeled, seeded, and diced
1 large red onion, diced
1½ celery stalks, thinly sliced
4 garlic cloves, minced
1 red bell pepper, seeded and diced
1 orange bell pepper, seeded and diced
1 large ripe tomato, seeded and diced
½ cup chopped fresh cilantro
1 tablespoon chopped fresh thyme
¼ cup fresh orange juice
Juice of 1 lemon
3 tablespoons olive oil
1 tablespoon red wine vinegar
Salt and pepper

Cook the rice in the broth according to the package directions. Cool to room temperature.

In a large serving bowl combine the rice with all of the other ingredients except the salt and pepper. Stir to combine, then season to taste.

Serves 8.

Peach Upside-Down Cake

5 plump peaches
8 tablespoons (1 stick) unsalted butter, softened
2 tablespoons amber crystal sugar or brown sugar
⅔ cup granulated sugar
1 egg
1 cup flour
¼ teaspoon salt
1 teaspoon baking powder
1 teaspoon vanilla extract
⅓ cup milk

Preheat oven to 350 degrees.

Blanch and peel the peaches. Cut them in eighths and remove the pits.

Grease the bottom and sides of a 9-inch nonstick baking pan with 2 tablespoons of the butter; sprinkle with 2 tablespoons of amber or brown sugar. Arrange the peach slices round side down in concentric circles to cover the bottom of the pan.

Beat the remaining 6 tablespoons of butter until fluffy. Add the granulated sugar and beat well. Continue mixing while adding the remaining ingredients. Pour the batter over the peaches and bake for 30 minutes. Remove the pan from the oven and cool the cake, in the pan, on a rack for 10 minutes. Put a serving plate over the pan and flip the cake onto the plate. If any peaches remain in the pan, carefully replace them on the cake.

Serves 8.

Grilled Mahimahi

Our dear friend Dr. Larry De Mann is an incredible chiropractor, and when he's not busy keeping us on our toes, he can often be found creating something delicious like this.

8 6-to-8-ounce fillets mahimahi
Juice of 4 lemons
1 tablespoon grated lemon zest
⅓ cup olive oil
4 cloves garlic, pressed
¼ cup chopped fresh basil
⅓ cup capers
Salt and pepper

Prepare grill.

Rinse the fish in cold water and pat dry with paper towels. Place the fish in a shallow dish.

In a bowl, whisk together the lemon juice, zest, olive oil, and garlic. Stir in the basil and capers. Season to taste. Let stand for 1 hour.

Coat the mahimahi generously with about half of the marinade. Grill the fish over a medium-high flame for 4 to 5 minutes per side. Place the cooked fish on a serving platter surrounded by the remainder of the marinade.

Serves 8.

Avocado, Snow Pea, and Walnut Salad

4 avocados, peeled, pitted, and diced
1½ cups snow peas, steamed and cooled
½ cup walnuts
8 cups mesclun
1 red onion, diced
¼ cup roasted pine nuts
1 tablespoon Dijon mustard
1 teaspoon sugar
2 tablespoons balsamic vinegar
4 tablespoons olive oil
Salt and pepper

In a large salad bowl, combine the avocados, snow peas, walnuts, lettuce, red onion, and pine nuts. In a small bowl, blend together the mustard, sugar, vinegar, oil, and salt and pepper to taste. Drizzle over salad and toss to coat.

Serves 6.

Heather's Mom's Lemon Meringue Pie

*T*his was my favorite dessert as a child. Even now, whenever I see a lemon meringue pie, I'm reminded of how much I love my mother and father.

CRUST

> ¾ cup vegetable shortening
> 1 tablespoon milk
> ¼ teaspoon salt
> 2 cups flour

In a bowl stir together the shortening and ¼ cup of boiling water until smooth. Add the milk and salt and stir to combine.

Place the flour in the bowl of a food processor. Add the shortening mixture and process until smooth. Form the dough into a ball, wrap it in waxed paper, then refrigerate it for 1 hour.

Preheat oven to 425 degrees.

Roll out the dough on a floured surface and transfer to a 9-inch pie plate. Trim the excess and crimp the edges. Fill the bottom of the shell with pie weights or dried beans. Bake for 16 to 18 minutes, until golden brown, and remove the weights or beans.

FILLING

> 1⅓ cups sugar
> ¼ cup corn starch
> 3 eggs, separated
> Grated rind of 1 lemon
> ¼ cup lemon juice
> 1 tablespoon butter

Turn oven to broil.

In a medium saucepan, combine 1 cup of sugar and the corn starch. Over medium-high heat, gradually stir in 1½ cups of cold water, then the lightly beaten egg yolks, and bring to a boil. Boil for 1 minute, then remove pan from the heat. Whisk in the lemon rind, lemon juice, and butter. Pour the filling into the crust.

With an electric mixer, beat the egg whites until foamy. Slowly beat in the remaining ⅓ cup of sugar until stiff peaks form. Spread the meringue evenly over the hot filling, covering it completely and touching the edge of the crust. Broil until meringue turns golden brown. Cool, then refrigerate.

Serves 8.

Roast Leg of Lamb

6-pound leg of lamb
3 tablespoons olive oil
6 garlic cloves, slivered
2 tablespoons chopped fresh rosemary (or 2 teaspoons dried)
2 tablespoons chopped fresh thyme (or 2 teaspoons dried)
1 tablespoon kosher salt
1 tablespoon cracked black peppercorns

Preheat even to 325 degrees.

Rinse the lamb under cold water and pat it dry with paper towels. Place it in a large roasting pan and brush it liberally with the olive oil. Make random slits in the meat with a paring knife and tuck the garlic slivers into the slits. Rub the herbs, salt, and pepper all over the lamb, pressing to stick.

Bake the lamb for 2 hours. Remove it from the oven and let it stand for 10 minutes before carving.

Serves 12.

Mint Chutney

1 bunch fresh mint
1 onion
Juice of 2 limes
4 tablespoons minced cilantro
½ teaspoon cayenne pepper
1½ teaspoons salt
1 tablespoon sugar

Rinse and dry the mint. Remove the leaves.

In a food processor or blender, combine the onion and lime juice, and puree. Add the mint leaves, cilantro, cayenne, salt, and sugar and blend. Chill.

Serves 6.

Cynthia's Potatoes

5 pounds Idaho potatoes, scrubbed and cut lengthwise like french-fries
8 tablespoons (1 stick) unsalted butter
Salt

Preheat oven to 500 degrees.

Divide the potatoes equally between two baking pans. Add enough water to cover the potatoes halfway. Dab 4 tablespoons of butter on each pan of potatoes. Salt liberally.

Bake until all of the water evaporates and the potatoes are crispy, about 45 minutes.

Serves 12.

Salad with Faux Benihana Vinaigrette

1 large head romaine lettuce or 2 heads Boston lettuce
3 tablespoons peanut oil
3 tablespoons walnut oil
2 tablespoons rice vinegar
2 tablespoons soy sauce
1 tablespoon minced fresh ginger
2 tablespoons sugar
Salt and pepper

Wash and dry the lettuce thoroughly. If using romaine, chop it into 1½-inch-wide strips.

In a food processor combine the oils, vinegar, soy sauce, ginger, and sugar, and mix well. Add salt and pepper to taste. Toss the dressing and lettuce together in a large bowl.

Serves 12.

Judy Tomkin's Almond Cake

A lovely and delightful cake, just like its namesake!

½ cup sliced almonds
1¼ cups cake flour (not self-rising)
¾ teaspoon baking powder
½ teaspoon baking soda
½ teaspoon salt
⅞ cup sugar
12 tablespoons (1½ sticks) unsalted butter, softened
⅔ cup sour cream
2 tablespoons heavy cream
2 eggs
1½ teaspoons almond extract
½ teaspoon vanilla extract
Powdered sugar

Preheat oven to 350 degrees.

Toast the sliced almonds on a baking sheet for about 8 minutes.

Butter a 9-inch round cake pan (preferably ceramic) and dust it with flour.

In the bowl of a large food processor combine the flour, baking powder, baking soda, and salt and process for 15 seconds. Add the almonds and sugar and process until the almonds are ground. Add the butter, sour cream, and heavy cream and process until just combined. Add the eggs, almond extract, and vanilla extract and process until smooth.

Pour the batter into the prepared pan. Bake for 35 to 40 minutes, until a toothpick comes out clean. Cool the pan on a rack, then turn the cake out onto a serving plate. Sprinkle with powdered sugar.

Serves 12.

Red Pepper and Fennel Soup

*T*his wonderful seasonal soup may be served hot, chilled, or at room temperature.

1 tablespoon unsalted butter

3 large red bell peppers, seeded and sliced

1½ large fennel bulbs, trimmed and diced (save green fronds for garnish)

3 medium leeks (white part only), washed and sliced thin

3 large Idaho potatoes, peeled and cut into chunks

2 quarts low-sodium or homemade chicken broth

Salt, white pepper, and cayenne pepper

½ cup whole milk

2 tablespoons Pernod

Heat the butter in the bottom of a large stockpot. Sauté the peppers, fennel, leeks, and potatoes for 5 minutes. Add the chicken broth and bring it to a boil. Reduce the heat and simmer, covered, for 30 minutes.

Transfer the soup to a food processor or blender (or use a hand-held blender) and puree. Return it to the pot and add salt, pepper and/or cayenne pepper to taste. Whisk in the milk and Pernod immediately before serving.

Serves 8.

Soft-Shell Crabs

12 soft-shell crabs, cleaned
2 lemons
½ cup white wine
¼ cup orange juice
1 teaspoon soy sauce
2 tablespoons cumin
3 garlic cloves, minced
3 tablespoons fresh ginger, minced
¼ teaspoon chili powder

In a large casserole dish, lay the crabs in a single layer and squeeze lemon juice over them.

In a small bowl combine all of the remaining ingredients. Pour the marinade over the crabs and marinate for at least 2 hours and as long as overnight.

Prepare the grill or preheat broiler.

Drain the marinade and cook the crabs for 5 minutes per side.

Serves 6.

Zucchini Gratin

3 medium to large zucchini or yellow squash, or both, scrubbed and
    sliced into ¼-inch rounds
2 tablespoons salt
3 tablespoons white wine
3 tablespoons balsamic vinegar
3 tablespoons olive oil
1 tablespoon fresh chopped thyme (or 1 teaspoon dried)
Salt and pepper

Place the zucchini in a strainer, toss with the salt, and drain for about 1
hour. This removes most of the water from the zucchini. Pat the rounds dry
with a paper towel, gently wiping off any excess salt.

Preheat oven to 350 degrees.

Arrange the zucchini in an overlapping pattern in an ovenproof baking
dish. In a small bowl combine the wine and vinegar with the olive oil,
thyme, and salt and pepper to taste (remember, the zucchini are already
pretty salty). Stir the vinaigrette briskly with a fork and pour it over the zucchini. Bake for 25 minutes.

Serves 6.

Fruit Cobbler

*L*eftover cobbler makes a delicious breakfast!

½ cup flour
¼ teaspoon salt
5 tablespoons unsalted butter, chilled
4 to 5 tablespoons ice water
6 cups fresh fruit (peaches, blueberries, apples, blackberries)
½ cup sugar
2 pints vanilla ice cream (optional)

Place the flour and salt in the bowl of the food processor and process for 10 seconds. Add the butter and process until the mixture is crumbly. Add the water 1 tablespoon at a time, pulsing after each addition, until the dough forms a ball. Turn out the ball onto waxed paper and chill for at least 30 minutes.

Preheat oven to 375 degrees.

Generously butter a 9-x-13-inch baking dish. Add the fruit and toss it to coat with sugar. Pinch off pieces of dough, flatten it into disks, and lay it on top of the fruit, roughly covering the surface.

Bake for 40 to 50 minutes, until the dough is golden. Serve immediately with the ice cream.

Serves 8.

Emergency Measures

Meatloaf can be incredibly versatile, as I found out one snowy January evening. The weather notwithstanding, I decided to have a little dinner in Connecticut. Our most beloved friend Hamilton South; his sister, our patient and adored editor Mary; and our lovely friend Lisa Cornelio came over from their nearby homes for what was meant to be a respite from nature's cruelty. They had all lost power, but our house seemed to be miraculously spared. Lisa was making her special version of rosemary and garlic potatoes, Hamilton brought a delicious beet salad and a gorgeous little raspberry tart from E.A.T. in New York, and I was preparing Jock's meatloaf, when disaster struck. The meatloaf and potatoes had been in the electric oven for only ten minutes when the house went black and the stereo went silent. As we searched for flashlights and frantically lit candles, we realized our dinner was in serious trouble. Hamilton and Damian sprang to the rescue! Braving the cold and frosty night, they retrieved the barbecue from its winter hibernation and set it up as close to the house as they could. The meatloaf and the potatoes were wrapped in foil, and we all wondered if this could really be done. It was not only edible but delicious, proving once again you can't go wrong with meatloaf.

SUMMER WEEKEND MENU

✤

DINNER
Cucumber Soup
Fried Chicken
Corn Salsa
Fresh Peach Pie

BREAKFAST
Panettone French Toast

LUNCH
Chicken Salad
Iceberg and Red Cabbage Salad
Fruit Salad

✤

We love our friends and love having lots of people around. The trick to making a weekend houseparty work, we've discovered, is to plan simple meals with recyclable components. In the dinner, breakfast, and lunch scenario that follows, for example, I'll fry lots of extra chicken so there are plenty of leftovers for the next day's chicken salad. I might serve a piece of blue cheese as an appetizer for dinner, then crumble what's left into the salad dressing at lunch. Extra peaches that didn't fit into the peach pie go into the fruit salad—you get the picture.

Serving meals family style helps keep the atmosphere casual. People can eat whenever they like, and we're freed up to spend more time with them.

J.S.

Cucumber Soup

6 large cucumbers, peeled and seeded (Set some aside for garnish.)
6 garlic cloves, crushed
5 tablespoons grated lemon rind
5 tablespoons lemon juice
12 cups plain yogurt
12 tablespoons chopped fresh chives
Salt and pepper
Paprika
1 bell pepper (red, orange, or yellow)

Place the first six ingredients in the bowl of a food processor or in a blender. Puree, then add salt and pepper to taste. Chill for 3 hours and garnish with paprika and thin slices of cucumber and diced bell pepper.

Serves 8 to 10.

Fried Chicken

When John Beal showed me how to make this fried chicken, he told me to marinate the chicken overnight, which I still do. If you haven't planned that far in advance, try to marinate for at least a couple of hours.

4 chicken breasts, halved

8 chicken legs

4 chicken thighs

6 cups buttermilk

8 garlic cloves, minced

1 teaspoon plus 1 tablespoon cumin

½ tablespoon cayenne pepper

Salt and pepper

3 to 4 cups vegetable oil

2½ cups flour

Rinse the chicken parts under cold water and pat them dry with paper towels. Place the chicken in a large dish. Add the buttermilk, garlic, 1 teaspoon cumin, cayenne, salt to taste, and plenty of pepper. Stir to combine the ingredients and coat the chicken. Cover and refrigerate overnight, if possible.

Preheat oven to 325 degrees.

Transfer the chicken and marinade to a roasting pan and place it in the oven. Bake for 30 to 45 minutes. Heather and I found this precooking technique yields really moist chicken with a nice crispy crust.

Remove the chicken from the oven and let it rest for 10 minutes. Heat the oil in a deep frying pan. Working in batches, dredge the chicken pieces in the flour mixed with the tablespoon of cumin, until they're heavily coated, then carefully place them in the frying pan (use tongs). When the pan is full, cover and cook over medium heat for 5 minutes. Remove the cover and cook for another 5 minutes, until the chicken begins to turn golden brown. Turn the chicken over and repeat: 5 minutes covered, 5 minutes uncovered. Transfer to a plate lined with paper towels, then repeat with the next batch.

Serves 16, or 8 with leftovers for the next day's lunch.

Corn Salsa

12 ears cooked corn
2 jalapeño peppers, red or green, diced
1 orange bell pepper, diced
1 red bell pepper, diced
1 large red onion, chopped
1 bunch fresh cilantro, chopped
Juice of 1½ lemons
3 tablespoons olive oil
4 garlic cloves, minced
Salt and pepper

Shave the kernels off the ears of corn into a large bowl. Add all of the remaining ingredients and mix well.

Serves 8.

Fresh Peach Pie

CRUST

    1½ cups vegetable shortening

    2 tablespoons milk

    ½ teaspoon salt

    4 cups flour

In a bowl stir together the shortening and ½ cup boiling water until smooth. Add the milk and salt and stir to combine.

Place the flour in the bowl of a food processor. Add the shortening mixture and process until smooth. Form the dough into two balls, wrap it in waxed paper, then refrigerate it for 1 hour.

FILLING

    4 cups fresh peaches, blanched, peeled, and sliced

    1 tablespoon lemon juice

    ¼ cup flour

    ½ cup sugar

    3 tablespoons butter

Preheat oven to 350 degrees.

Roll out one dough ball and transfer it to a 9-inch pie plate. Trim the edges.

In a large bowl combine the peach slices, lemon juice, flour, and sugar. Pour the mixture into the crust. Dot the top of the peaches with 2 tablespoons of the butter.

Roll out the remaining dough ball and transfer it to the top of the pie. Crimp the edges and make 3 or 4 slits in the top crust (for steam to escape). Melt the remaining butter and paint the crust with it using a pastry brush.

Place the pie pan on a cookie sheet in the oven (it's easier to clean a cookie sheet than an oven). Bake for 1 hour, until the crust is golden brown.

Serve warm or at room temperature, accompanied by whipped cream or vanilla ice cream.

Serves 8.

Panettone French Toast

$\mathcal{P}$anettone is a delicious light, sweet Italian cake. It comes in a box and is usually available in gourmet stores. If you can't find it, any other eggy sweet bread will do, such as challah or brioche.

1 panettone (1 pound, 1.6 ounces; or 500 grams)
2 eggs
½ cup milk
8 tablespoons (1 stick) unsalted butter
Maple syrup

Preheat oven to 250 degrees.

Slice the panettone into 16 slices. Place the eggs and milk in a bowl and stir with a fork to combine. Melt 1 tablespoon of butter in a skillet over medium heat. Dip both sides of a slice of panettone in the egg mixture, then lay it in the pan. Repeat with another slice and more butter. Cook until the underside is golden, about 3 minutes, then flip. When the second side is golden, remove the slice from the pan and place it in an ovenproof dish. Put the dish in the oven to keep the toast warm.

Repeat, adding butter as necessary, until all the panettone is cooked. Serve each person 2 slices and pass warm maple syrup.

Serves 8.

Chicken Salad

Y ou can use any kind of leftover chicken in this salad—fried, roasted, grilled. (If you don't have leftovers, boil some boneless chicken until the meat is white all the way through). Make the salad a couple of hours in advance, to give the flavors a chance to blend.

3 to 4 pounds leftover cooked chicken
1 large red onion, diced
5 celery stalks, sliced thin
1 tablespoon chopped fresh tarragon (or 1 teaspoon dried)
½ cup Hellmann's mayonnaise
3 tablespoons Dijon mustard
Salt and pepper

Cut the chicken into bite-sized pieces and place it in serving bowl. Add all of the other ingredients and toss to mix and coat. Adjust the seasonings, then toss again. Refrigerate until ready to serve.

Serves 8.

Iceberg and Red Cabbage Salad

We got the idea for this salad from a restaurant in New York called Main Street. Our friend Steven Scherr owns this gold mine, which specializes in comfort food served family style—meatloaf and mashed potatoes, fried chicken, lasagna—just like Mom makes it. Main Street serves only iceberg; we add red cabbage to make the salad more colorful. Feel free to experiment with the greens of your choice.

1 head iceberg lettuce, diced
1 small red cabbage, diced
½ cup fresh blue cheese, crumbled
1 cup low-fat mayonnaise or plain yogurt

Place the lettuce and cabbage in a large serving bowl. In a small bowl, mix the blue cheese and mayonnaise or yogurt. Pour the dressing over the salad, toss, chill for 20 minutes, and serve.

Serves 8 to 10.

Fruit Salad

5 cups mixed fresh fruit: peeled, sliced peaches, nectarines, mangoes;
  sliced bananas; berries; halved grapes; melon balls
½ cup fresh orange juice
2 tablespoons chopped crystallized ginger

Combine all of the ingredients in a large bowl. Toss and serve.

Serves 8.

INDEX